The New Legacy Expanded

by Tonja K. Taylor

POWERLight Learning
Ft. Worth, Texas

"Because what you read matters!"

10 For as the rain and snow come down from the heavens, and return not there again, but water the earth and make it bring forth and sprout, that it may give seed to the sower and bread to the eater, 11 So shall My word be that goes forth out of My mouth: it shall not return to Me void [without producing any effect, useless], but it shall accomplish that which I please *and* purpose, and it shall prosper in the thing for which I sent it. - Isaiah 55:10-11, AMPC

---

1. http://www.Lockman.org

2. https://creativecommons.org/publicdomain/zero/1.0/

3. https://biblehub.com/

4. https://discoverybible.com/

5. https://openbible.com/

6. https://creativecommons.org/publicdomain/zero/1.0/

Print ISBN: 978-1-965641- 26-2

Ebook ISBN: 978-1-965641-25-5

We pray the LORD will use this book as a powerful catalyst in the life of your family to deepen your love and understanding of His Word, and cause the light in you to go forth in the darkness so that others may see and draw closer to Jesus, the True Life.

Remember, all our efforts bring a profit—especially speaking the living Word of God (Prov. 14:23-24)!

Table of Contents

Reviews of Legacy

"As a parent of three kids living in such a negative generation, it is refreshing to read in Legacy that parents can positively shape their child's destiny through the power of the spoken Word of God. Legacy is not to be read as a novel or newspaper article, but as a study tool to help parents, like myself, craft the gift of life that God has placed within their home." —Pastor Steve Crowder, Founder/President, High Way Ministries Int'l, Boulder, Colorado

"Thank you for the kind mention regarding the eCover. I'm afraid I didn't make it very far into the book yet. Let me explain. While reading the First Things First section, I was touched by the section on baptism of the Holy Spirit. This is something I've been struggling with for a long time. Like you, I was raised not believing in this, but have been questioning it for a long time. Thank you for sharing your story. I'm not ready yet to pray the prayer you wrote, but if/when I am, I appreciate knowing right where to find it. Thank you for letting me preview your book. It has already been a blessing and I'm just getting started!"—Mike Smith, (first Legacy cover designer).

"As parents and grandparents, we have an obligation to train up our children in the ways of the Lord. Tonja has given us a powerful tool and training platform to begin doing just that. As you pray words of Faith, Worship, Wisdom and Destiny over your children, it will also stir and build your faith. Legacy has a lot of wealth in it, but it is not a book that is read. It is a resource; as such it must be used repeatedly so that the riches that lie within are sown to our future generations."—David E. Andrews, Wall Street, New York

"The content and concept of Legacy were great. I thought the cover was superb. What better way to protect our precious children from harm than the all-powerful sword that is God's Word. If we go into "battle" without our sword, we are doomed to fall in battle, or at least take a terrible beating along the way."—Dr. Kim F. veterinarian, 45, Sunday-School teacher 7-12 grade at a church in Texas

"I got it and love it. I was just going to glance through it because I did not have but a few minutes to look at it but I just could not put it down. I love the format and the font is big enough to read easily. There were some of the Scriptures that I had not thought to pray over loved ones and some of the Scriptures that I was not familiar with. I already can think of three people that I want to share it with. I am blessed to be a prayer partner and friend to you." –Becky B, 66, retired veteran teacher, Arkansas

Preface

"...The Father is with Me. I've told you all this so that trusting Me, you will be unshakable and assured, deeply at peace. In this godless world you will continue to experience difficulties. But take heart! I've conquered the world."—John 16:32, 33, The Message

As a Believer in the LORD Jesus Christ Who has repented of one's sin and received Christ Jesus as Savior and LORD (John 3:15-17; Romans 10:23), you have the power to speak God's eternal, unchanging, life-saving Truth over your child(ren)—and shape their lives for the Kingdom of God.

You can also speak the Word over yourself, your spouse, your relatives, your co-workers, your church family, the government, and more—to bring healing, deliverance, freedom; and salvation, direction, and more (John 8:31-32, Rom. 10:9)!

In these times of dangerous deception and confusion, it is vital that we teach our children (who are more morally-challenged than all previous generations!) the importance of the Word of God, and that we speak the Word—the real Truth—over them.

The Word of God created the world (John 1:1-4), and what we say has a major impact on our lives and our loved ones (Prov. 18:21; Mark 11:23-24). When we are true Believers in Christ, then the same creative power of words lives in us! We can speak the Word of God, knowing it is always working (Isaiah 55:10-11) as we say it!

Tonja K. Taylor has proven this in her own life, by blessing her own daughter and other children (students in public and private schools and online, as well as other kids she has ministered to through the decades), and shaping their lives by speaking the Word to and over them, directly and through prayer.

This book, which came out of a 6-week class the LORD mandated Tonja to teach in 2006 at a pro-life pregnancy center, will help you learn to find Scriptures to help transform your life and your loved ones for good—*for God!*

Although the impact of speaking His Word cannot be measured till Heaven, saying what God says is one of the most important use of the gift of speech there is! By faith, we know that He watches over His Word to perform it (Jer. 1:12), and His angels listen to and act on His Word (Psalm 103:20)! Hallelujah!

The New Legacy Expanded has many more pages of material to encourage you to never stop speaking God's Word over your child(ren), yourself, and others. Christ Jesus the King is returning very soon, and we must be ready!

One potential reader (a man in his late 40s), when I told him of my first vision for the *Legacy* book cover, gasped and said, "A sword and children don't go together! What will people think?!"

(The cover of the original book, *Legacy: Crafting Your Child's Future With Words*, published in 2007, had a picture of a mighty sword, and the Mightiest Sword—the Word of God—on it).

He almost got it.

The point is, *we must think—and understand!*

We must understand.

We must understand that our children, if they are to not only survive but thrive, must fight.

They must fight with wisdom.

They must fight with power.

They must fight with the victorious Word of God.

And we must teach them.

But in order to teach, we first must learn.

"...a miracle is no cute thing but more like the swing of a sword....We and the world, my children, will always be at war. Retreat is impossible. Arm yourselves."—Leif Enger, *Peace Like a River*

Let the New Legacy begin!

Dedication

To all those seeking ZOE life, no matter their calling, who long to know more of the majesty and goodness of our Father God as they live to please Him, and teach their children to love His Word—thus promoting the life of God to them, and through them.

"...be strong, all ye people of the land, saith the LORD, and work: for I am with you, saith the LORD of hosts. According to the word that I covenanted with you when you came out of Egypt, so My Spirit remaineth among you: fear ye not." —Hag. 2:4b-5

"And they shall teach My people the difference between the holy and profane, and cause them to discern between the unclean and the clean." —Eze. 44:23

"Get up! Cry out at night, every hour on the hour. Pour your heart out like water in the presence of the LORD. Lift up your hand to Him (in prayer) for the life of your little children who faint from (spiritual) hunger at every street corner." —Lam. 2:19 (God's Word Translation)

We win, with God's Word in our mouths!

As for Me, this is My covenant or league with them, says the Lord: My Spirit, Who is upon you [and Who writes the law of God inwardly on the heart], and My words which I have put in your mouth shall not depart out of your mouth, or out of the mouths of your [true, spiritual] children, or out of the mouths of your children's children, says the Lord, from henceforth and forever. – Isaiah 59:21, AMPC

But this is the covenant which I will make with the house of Israel: After those days, says the Lord, I will put My law within them, and on their hearts will I write it; and I will be their God, and they will be My people. – Jeremiah 31:33, AMPC

For this is the covenant that I will make with the house of Israel after those days, says the Lord: I will imprint My laws upon their minds, even upon their innermost thoughts and understanding, and engrave them upon their hearts; and I will be their God, and they shall be My people. – Hebrews 8:10, AMPC

This is the agreement (testament, covenant) that I will set up and conclude with them after those days, says the Lord: I will imprint My laws upon their hearts, and I will inscribe them on their minds (on their inmost thoughts and understanding), He then goes on to say, And their sins and their lawbreaking I will remember no more. – Hebrews 10:16-17, AMPC

Thanks and Acknowledgements

I thank my God always on your behalf, for the grace of God which is given you by Jesus Christ. —I Corinthians 1:4

First, I must thank King Jesus, Who has mandated that I write and make many books! (Matthew 13:52; Romans 5:19). He is glorious and victorious and worthy of all our praise, and His Word has saved me from certain death in every realm. He has redeemed me, and set me on the Rock of Himself with a new song on my mouth. I pray every word in this book is anointed and blessed by Him.

Next is my darling dynamite husband, Mr. Clayton Taylor. He has been second only to Jesus as my constant encourager, support, and prayer cover, doing everything he could to help me succeed, including editing the written and audio versions of Legacy. God has used him to give me confidence and liberty, and a much deeper understanding of the agape love of God. This highly anointed man has much wisdom to share with the world. I love working with you and look forward to many more projects together, my Wise Darling Man!

My precious daughter, Victoria, is truly a delight and inspiration, and very talented and creative in her own right. It is a thrill to work with her to create works that serve as catalysts for Christ in the hearts of all who experience these efforts!

I also appreciate all the family and loved ones, including ministries and others who have prayed for me to finish these projects the LORD has called me to, and distribute them where they should go, so the LORD can shoot them like mighty arrows to hit their targets! Amen.

Also, thank you, dear reader, for reading and sharing this book. When you invest in the Word of God, you are helping yourself and all those you know!

ZOE to you all!

How to Use This Book

The fear of the LORD is pure, enduring forever. The ordinances of the LORD are sure and altogether righteous. They are more precious than gold, than much pure gold; they are sweeter than honey, than honey from the comb. By them is your servant warned; in keeping them there is great reward.—Psalm 19:9-11 (NIV)

When I started writing this book and was choosing Scriptures to pray as blessings over children,

it seemed I should copy the entire Bible except perhaps a few verses in the Old Testament and some of the more complex ones in Revelation!

As one highly esteemed pastor said that God told him once, "It's all good!"

Talk Like Jesus

There is nothing more precious than the Word. It is eternal, magnificent, matchless, and alive. It is sublime. And if you are saved by faith in the atoning death of Christ Jesus when He spilled His priceless blood on the cross for you to enjoy divine health and freedom from the penalty of your sins, then you are one with Jesus, Who is the eternal Word (John 1:1). When you speak God's Word, the enemy hears Jesus talking. Hallelujah!

It is the same with your children. As they accept and grow in Christ and learn to wield the incredible authority we believers have when speaking God's Word, they will also continue the plan of God—to destroy the works of the enemy. So the more we parents talk like Jesus—speak the Word—to and over our kids, the more powerfully we shape their destinies for Him and set the example for them to sharpen and swing their own Swords!

Shape the Future of Your Child

In The Message Bible, Hebrews 11:18 states, **"By faith, Isaac reached into the future as he blessed Jacob and Esau."**

When the patriarchs blessed (invoked the blessing upon their children by speaking specific words about their future, it produced eternal impact—for good or not. According to Webster's dictionary, some of the meanings of "blessing" are "The act or words of a person who blesses,"

"The invocation of God's favor upon a person," or "approval," so we see that even the secular writers of this authority on words, the dictionary, recognize the power of them.

As one minister says, "Blessing your children is 'results-oriented praying.'" Amen.

The time is short; whatever age your children are (even grown!), the seeds of the Word planted in them can only bear fruit! Glory to God!

I know He is pleased with the Word that I've planted in my daughter Victoria (now 27, married 4 years to her best friend that she met at church camp about 15 years ago, and doing very well!). Hallelujah!

I have spoken the Word over her daily in prayer and otherwise, for all these years (even when she was in the womb, and I dedicated her to the LORD at church, when she was three months old, on Mother's Day!).

Yet I must not stop there; the planting of His Word into her (and the many other children I've had, as a teacher in public and private schools, online, and in church and other community organizations the past 40+ years!) is a daily privilege, task, and joy.

It is a joy for you when you sow (plant) it into your children and other loved ones! Our delight is in our giving—whether financial, material, emotional, spiritual, or otherwise (Acts 25:35). Hallelujah!

Proverbs 1:5 states that **"The wise also will hear and increase in learning, and the person of understanding will acquire skill and attain to sound counsel (so that he may be able to steer his course rightly)."**

It is never too early nor too late to start a deeper study of the Scriptures, for the Word will accomplish that for which it is sent (Isa. 55:11).

Even when my daughter was in my womb, I was praying over her and singing praise songs to her, and holding her while "we" danced to true worship songs.

It is well known that babies can hear before they are born, so if you are expecting, do not think your efforts will be wasted if you speak the Word to your baby-to-be! Words have power, and as soon as they are released, they affect our lives and others'—for evil or for good.

Dedicate Your Child to the LORD

Another idea is to dedicate your child to the LORD, as I did on Mother's Day when she was three months old. God led me to carefully choose Scriptures to be proclaimed over her then. Many of them I still speak over her daily (as she grew up, even calling her on the phone to speak them, if she wasn't with me, and daily now that she's married! I speak them over her spouse too, and many others, of course. I now have many spiritual children, including the hundreds of students I've taught in-person and online, through the years in public school, church, community, and more!)

Faith comes by hearing, and hearing by the Word of God (Rom.10:17). As you bless your children, remember that not only will the eternal Word go forth to start shaping your child's life to the glory of God, it will soothe and strengthen your faith, drawing you closer to Him, and otherwise work in your life to create the wise, victorious, loving, peaceful, joyful mother (or father) that you long to be.

How to be a Master Gardener

In Matthew 17:20 and Luke 17:6, Jesus compares our faith in His Word to a seed. One pastor said that the reason He chose the mustard seed is that it absolutely remains pure. It cannot be cross-pollinated.

So I have a question for you: What kinds of seeds are you planting in the tender gardens that are your children? Are you planting the

Word? (I may be mixing metaphors since the thrust of the book compares the Word to a sword, but I'll use whatever I can to help you understand the importance of speaking the Word to and over your kids!)

The Word is the mightiest seed on earth, and like all seeds that produce nourishing, life-giving fruit, it must be planted on purpose, then watered and tended and kept.

Be assured that you are continuously planting seeds in your children, every day, for good or bad. These seeds are planted not only by what we do and say to and for them, but by who and what we allow in our children's lives. Be aware that "others" are also busy planting seeds in your kids.

"Others" include teachers at school and at church; friends; relatives; television; video and computer games; magazines; music; books, toys, and more.

The enemy is often more avid a gardener than we are, and is constantly scheming to plant the wrong seeds (called "tares" in the Word, Matt. 13:25-40) in our children. We must guard them with the Sword of the Spirit and teach them to guard their hearts.

Of course, we remember and rejoice that the enemy is defeated by the victory of Jesus on the cross 2,000 years ago! That victory is ours when we live in Him by believing, acting upon, and speaking His Word.

That victory is passed to our children as we diligently plant and water the precious seeds of the Word into them. In addition, everything else we say shapes their lives. If we speak negatively, gossiping, complaining, being sarcastic, we should not wonder why they act the same way (Phil. 2:14, Jam. 5:9).

If we have a thankful heart and express thanks with joy continually (Eph. 5:20), they will follow that example. May the LORD pour grace upon our lips, and cause our words to be gently firm and consistent, motivated by love, as we honor His children that we have been given to train.

How to Use Legacy

The New Legacy Expanded is written in short chapters for easy reading, but it is not intended to replace the daily Bible reading you and your children already do. It is more like vitamins; like taking vitamins to supplement daily meals. Too many vitamins or good food can be bad for you, but feast without end to your best health on the Word.

Remember: "It's all good!" and you cannot overdose on the Word of God!

Use the blank space and your Bible; write them out and make them yours. Get a notebook for yourself, and one for each of your children. Let them see you write the Word and speak it, and have them do the same. Let them illustrate the Word, or draw "doodles," or whatever works to engage them with as many senses as possible! When you finish this book, you'll have a unique, priceless treasure of The Word!

God's Word is written to us as a personal love letter, so go deeper in the Word and let Him love on you and help you love your children—for life! You will wonder why you waited so long to do so!

Personally, I have found it hard to discard any piece of paper with the Word of God written on it, no matter how wrinkled or ragged, when there are so many in the world that would treasure such a scrap, with the life-changing Word!

So a few years ago, I empathized when I read that the Hebrews that copy the Scriptures refuse to throw away a piece of paper with the words of YHWH (Yahweh, the Hebrew name for Jehovah) on it.

The Bible is precious and priceless, and there are many hungry people in other countries that would love to feast on even one of those ragged papers on which is written the Word of life! (One way to reach others who are hungry for the Word is to share your resources, such as Bibles, CDs, DVDs, magazines, and more by sending them to LovePackages.org. They and others (MissionCry.com) collect these materials and ship them overseas to many countries—including some "under the radar"!)

In addition, as you explore the Word on your own and think of other things you want to pray about for your child, don't worry about whether the verses you choose have the actual subject words (i.e., faith, worship) in them; go with God. If the Holy Spirit speaks to you about a certain verse, it doesn't matter what "category" it's in here, or even how it's listed in the index of your Bible.

Just write it down and start speaking it over your child. Listen to God. He knows what we need much more than we do. Have faith that, even when we don't understand something, He is faithful to guide us. He is so good! Praise Him!

Oh, the depth of the riches and wisdom and knowledge of God! How unfathomable (inscrutable, unsearchable) are His judgments (His decisions)! And how untraceable (mysterious, undiscoverable) are His ways (His methods, His paths)! – Romans 11:33, AMPC

Scriptures to Go

It's easy to make your own treasure cards of Scriptures. Buy regular notecards (especially those brightly-colored ones), blank business card stock, or just cut out your own from whatever paper you can find and write those verses on them, and put them in your children's lunch. Have your kids write and illustrate them. Victoria (and some of my sweeties in the Christian kindergarten I taught, along with my dear kiddos in 1-6 grade church classes) did that, and I still haves some of those jewels!

Discuss them. Read them in context (in the midst of the many verses around them, to get the right feel for how they are meant in the Bible). Draw your own pictures, or let the kids decorate them. Put on music that glorifies the LORD, silly songs that are not tacky, or instrumental music, and speak the Word out loud; some children learn better when memorizing to music.

The point is to pour the living water of the Word into your family! Of course, please pray as you read this book, and thank the LORD that He will use it to strengthen your faith and eternally shape the lives of your child(ren). There are many ways to learn the Word of God, so dig in and enjoy.

Feel free to print out the whole book, or any of the pages for your personal use. The Scriptures are from one of the versions listed in the front of this book. All other writing than the Scriptures are © Tonja K. Taylor, POWERLight Learning.

Use the Reward System

Using rewards for learning a certain number of verses is something that might work to help your kids enjoy the process even more. Also, programs where the children are taught Bible verses are excellent.

My only concern is that, experientially, I have discovered that the emphasis in such clubs on earning points to have a winning team can cause a rushing through saying the Word, rather than making sure the children hide them in their heart so they might not sin against God. However, the more children are exposed to God's Word, especially in an enjoyable atmosphere, the more they will find it "sweeter than honey and more precious than gold." (Psalm 19:10).

Still, the ultimate responsibility for teaching the Word to the children and proclaiming it over them is ours as parents. As I have sought creative ways to teach the Word to my daughter, this book and the Scripture card ideas were born.

Every day, when I homeschooled Victoria, Bible would be our first subject. Sometimes, it would go for more than an hour, over breakfast! I'd let her illustrate the Scriptures, and I still have those precious original works of art!

We proclaim the Word as prayers to the LORD, Who is faithful to hear and answer (Prov. 15:29, Psm 3:4) and work in the lives of our children in response to our faith. And as my dynamite little daughter said in Tulsa when she was four (after I had rocked and prayed and sang over her and thought she was asleep), "Don't stop pwayin', Mama!"

Just a few (it seems) years ago, I handed that same 10-year-old daughter a list of verses on a subject I'd had to correct her about and requested that she read them aloud. She did, then smiled at me, gazed into my eyes, and said, "Mama, I'm glad I'm growing up like this."

Praise the LORD, that is priceless—and so worth it all!

"Therefore, my beloved brethren, be firm (steadfast), immovable, always abounding in the work of the LORD, knowing and being continually aware that your labor in the LORD is not futile (it is never wasted or to no purpose)." –I Cor. 15:57, 57, AMP

As our Master, LORD Jesus said, **"Heaven and earth shall pass away, but My words shall not pass away."**—Matt. 24:35, KJV

GOD BLESS YOU and MORE POWER TO YOU!

How This Book Will Help You

While every born-again believer should be under the continual teaching of a pastor who fully follows God's Holy Bible, LEGACY will assist in helping you learn to use the Word to protect your children from the enemy, to give them the God life instead of just "the good life," and to shape them to become mighty lights for the LORD—for which they were sent here by God.

First Things First

The thief comes only in order to steal and kill and destroy. I (JESUS) came that they may have and enjoy life, and have it in abundance (to the full, till it overflows).—John 10:10, AMP, emphasis mine

As the Apostle Paul said, if you have not received Jesus Christ as your Savior, you will not fully

understand this Book. Spiritual truths are hidden from those without the living Christ within, helping them to understand (I Cor. 2:14).

The Heart of the Matter

You are an eternal being. Like every person, you were born into sin, because of the error of God's first children in the Garden of Eden (Gen. 3) When your body dies, it will dissolve to dirt again (Gen. 3:19), but your spirit will live forever—in Heaven with God (Rom. 8:31-39, Col. 1:20-22), or hell, eternally separated from Him (Luke 16:22-29).

The Word is real. It is a living Book. It is a love letter and instruction manual from God, the Creator and Sustainer (Isa. 42:5), and Savior of all life and giver of all good things (Isa. 45:21, 22). God sent His only Son, Jesus, to live a sinless life on earth then die on the cross to pay for all our wrongs, so we don't have to (John 3:16). We can either reject that matchless gift, or receive it. It is a choice, and the most important we will make in our lives.

The choice we must make is whether to take God at His Word—that we need a Savior and He has provided that One, or to live under the lie that either (a) we don't need a Savior and will just "go to sleep" or dissolve or something when our heart stops beating; or (b) that we will all be accepted into Heaven, because God is Love and why would He send anyone to hell, or (c) that we can do enough good things to be accepted to get in.

All assumptions that we don't need a Savior are wrong! Jesus said in John 14:6 that He is "the Way, the Truth and the Life." No person gets into Heaven except by Him. He is the Door (John 10:9).

But once you understand that you need Jesus and you receive His free and eternal gift of salvation by grace (we can't earn it!) through faith, then the LORD comes to live inside of you as the Holy Spirit, to continue to teach and lead you into the wonderful abundant life of God, called "Zoe" in Greek. Old things pass away, for the LORD makes all things new (Isa. 43:18,19). When you receive Him, you are born again in the Spirit; you become a new creation, which is the only thing that counts (2 Cor. 5:17). We all like a fresh start, and that's what Jesus gives—Ultimate New Life!

If you want a wonderful, rich, abundant new life today, please say the following prayer, focusing on a loving Savior Who has His arms extended to you right now to welcome you into the Family of God:

Heaven is Just a Sincere Prayer Away!

Dear Jesus, I believe that You died for my sins, and rose again to eternal life. I need You as my Savior. I ask You to forgive me of all my sins, to come and live in my heart and help me live for You. I thank You for the abundant life You will bring me as You teach me to walk in Your ways. I thank You that by Your blood, I will be set free from past sins and given grace and strength to become a new creation in You. I receive You now, LORD Jesus! Thank You! AMEN.

And There's More!

Then there is the baptism of the Holy Spirit, the next step in becoming supernaturally effective as a witness for the LORD; it is the most precious gift after salvation, and free as is salvation to all who will receive it (Luke 11:13, Acts 2). The saved person who wisely chooses to receive the filling of the Holy Spirit then becomes a vessel through which the Spirit of God can do miracles!

The greater reward of being filled with the Holy Spirit is the sublime experience of intimate interaction with the LORD, now your loving Abba Father, your Daddy God (Rom. 8:14-17)—feeling, seeing, and hearing His loving Voice and His priceless Spirit much deeper and more powerfully than before!

He is always ready to give to you, including this great power for His service. There is no waiting in line for audience with Him, for those who are sincere (I Chron. 28:9). Jesus died and rose again that He might return to Heaven, having finished His work, and in order to send the Holy Spirit.

His Spirit is everywhere at once in this world, drawing all Who will listen to new life in Christ. Jesus the Holy Spirit longs to communicate with you continuously and be your very best Friend, Savior,

Helper, Teacher, Encourager, Defender, Protector, Provider, Guide and Glory (John 14:26)!

HALLELUJAH! Jesus, The King will soon return, and bring His reward with Him (Rev. 22:12). So let us be empowered and found being about His business (I Cor. 15:58)! Remember, the closer you are to God, the closer you will be able to lead your dear children to Him.

If you wish to take the very next step and receive the baptism of the Holy Spirit with the evidence of speaking in tongues (Acts 2:1-11, 2:37-41), please say the following prayer. Remember that God empowers willing people to do miracles and experience the depth of His love and favor in supernatural ways the same today as He did over 2,000 years ago.

As He says in Malachi 3:6, **"I AM the LORD; I change not,"** and **"Jesus Christ the same yesterday, and today, and forever."** (Heb. 13:8). Now, please pray this to be empowered by God for greater service to Him:

For Real Power From On High!

Dear Father in Heaven,

I thank You that You give us all good things. I thank You that the miracles You did over 2000 years ago, You still do today, for You never change. Now that I have received by faith what Your Son Jesus did for me

on the cross and have become Your child, I ask that You baptize me in the Holy Spirit so that I may feel Your sweet Presence daily; so that I may hear and see and experience You in ways I never have before; and so that You may do miracles through me and change this world for good—for God! In Jesus name, I receive You, Holy One! AMEN.

Now, yield to Him; allow the Holy Spirit to speak through you—the beautiful language of His Spirit, which is unique to you! If this does not happen immediately, do not become discouraged. It will happen; His Spirit will flow through you—if you want it to! God is a Gentleman, and never forces His will on anyone (Otherwise, every human ever born would be born again into Christ!)

For Skeptics

Growing up as a Southern Baptist, I did not believe in the baptism, or "filling," of the Holy Spirit. I thought that and healing were fake and from hell and even made fun of both. (I have repented, of course.) But the LORD knew I wanted it to be real.

He also knew I wanted to be a vessel through which He worked to change this world. So He led me to teaching resources by Spirit-filled Christians like the book The Wonderful Spirit-Filled Life4 by Dr. Charles Stanley. God also led me to Christian friends who seemed just like me, only who spoke in English then in their Spirit languages as the Holy Spirit led.

Still skeptical, I finally challenged a Tulsa pastor by asking him, "How do you make God speak through you?!" He replied that when one was baptized in the Holy Spirit, one did not make God speak, one just opened one's mouth and allowed the Power that was already there to come out—like putting a plug into an electric socket to allow the current to flow through and make something happen!

A close friend in Tulsa whom I knew loved God demonstrated speaking in tongues when I asked and was just otherwise a "normal" person. So, through all of this, the LORD convinced me that I should give it a try—what did I have to lose?

Hungry for more of the living God, I decided I'd give it a shot. When I first prayed with a couple at church June 11, 2000, to receive the Holy Spirit, nothing happened.

I was disappointed, but the LORD gave me peace, and I told Him, "Father, it's all in Your time. When You want it to happen, I know it will." After church, I bought a hamburger and went home. I was sitting at the table eating, and the LORD said, "Put down your sandwich and stand up."

A New Life!

A great sense of expectancy rose in me. I smiled and raised my hands to Him and said, "Father, loose my tongue!" And He did. At first, it was just a few words that He spoke through me, and then my new language started flowing like a river. From then on, I started thinking even more like God; I wanted to read the Bible more, understand more, be in His presence more.

That, of course, is His goal; He is to be our focus. He is to be our lives!

The baptism of the Holy Spirit has many advantages: When I "feel" discouraged or doubtful or confused (we can't trust feelings!), I pray in the Spirit. And I worship. I open my mouth and praise—from singing, to shouting His victorious Word, and very soon my mind is on Him, where it's supposed to be (Isa.26:3).

I open my mouth and start talking, and the LORD fills my mouth with His words, so that I pray mysteries, the perfect will of God (I Cor. 14:2). I pray when I need wisdom, and, often after just minutes of praying in the Spirit, I have the answer. Sometimes, too, I will pray in the Spirit and then pray out in English what I need to know.

Sometimes as I pray in the Spirit, or sing in the Spirit (what a comfort to know that, in the Spirit, my voice sounds so beautiful to the LORD!), He will bring a name to mind of someone I haven't thought of in years, but who needs my prayer at that moment.

I could be praying for the victory of a saint on the other side of the world, for my family's blessing and deeper walk with God, for my pastor's insight, for a co-worker's salvation, for world events, or anything else God wants. It doesn't matter. What matters is that I am a willing vessel and I allow God to get done what He wants to through me.

Also since being filled with the Spirit—which I wish I'd understood and received a couple decades ago!—I understand the Bible better. My joy, peace, love, prayers, and praise are deeper. I feel Him very quickly respond to my worship, because through His Spirit, I worship Him truly (John 4:23). I also have a better grasp of who I am in Christ, the love He has for me (I Jn 4:16), and the availability and greatness of His power working in and for me. And you can too.

You have nothing to lose and Heaven to gain.

As author John R. Stott said, "To follow Christ is to renounce all lesser loyalties."

Introduction and Background

"And the words of the LORD are flawless, like silver refined in a furnace of clay, purified seven times."—Psalm 12:6

According to one pastor, "The work of Jesus Christ is finished. He's already done all He is going to do." The rest is up to us. If we want the future to be better, it is our responsibility to shape our children to be their spiritual best, by harnessing the power of our words.

Words Carry Extreme Power

One minister says, "Our words are containers." So we must be aware and extremely concerned about what they contain, for the words we speak directly affect our children's lives and our own.

As Dan Stratton, Pastor of Faith Exchange Fellowship in New York states in his book, *Divine ProVision: Positioning God's Kings for Financial Conquest*, "...you and I are created in (God's) image and...by design created also to speak our future into existence....That is why God has told us to speak things that are in agreement with Him—and that we will be judged one day for those times when we have not." (Mal. 3:13,14; Matt. 12:37)

We parents have the duty and privilege to speak the Word of God over our children daily—both defensively and offensively. Our enemy the devil was defeated over 2000 years ago by King Jesus, Hallelujah! By speaking the Word of God, we enforce that defeat, and we liberate the LORD to perfect His plan in the lives of those we love.

It is an easy, enjoyable, and empowering thing to choose to speak the Word over our children daily.

We also have this marvelous, heart-thrilling promise in Isaiah 59:21 (NASB95) from our Father, the Most High God, about His Word for us and our children: **"As for Me, this is My covenant with them," says the LORD: "My Spirit which is upon you, and My words which I have put in your mouth shall not depart from your mouth, nor from the mouth of your offspring, nor from the mouth** of your offspring's offspring," says the LORD, "from now and forever."

Hallelujah! However, this will not just happen! We must be deliberate in speaking the Word to and over our children (no matter how young or old they are); it is a lifetime Assignment!

Then the LORD can work with our efforts, for just believing is not enough in this case; we must put effort into this—just like we put effort into anything that we think is worthwhile. From mowing the grass to brushing our teeth, to working for money, to sharing information and material goods with others, etc., we have to do something for these things to be accomplished, and the LORD is so good!

He will help us!

"For the Lord GOD helps Me, Therefore, I am not disgraced; Therefore, I have made My face like flint, And I know that I will not be ashamed."—Isa. 50:7, NASB

So I answered them and said to them, "The God of heaven will make us successful; therefore we His servants will arise and build, but you (enemy) have no part, right, or memorial in Jerusalem." – Neh. 2:20, NASB, emphasis mine

6[1] Blessed be the LORD, Because He has heard the sound of my pleading. 7[2] The LORD is my strength and my shield; My heart trusts in Him, and I am helped; Therefore my heart triumphs, And with my song I shall thank Him.—Psa. 28:6-7, NASB

For clearly He does not give help to angels, but He gives help to the descendants of Abraham (us!). – Heb. 2:16, NASB, emphasis mine.

Believers Today Are Kings and Priests

In the Old Testament, a father's blessing was priceless, so prized that it could cause men to scheme to steal the blessing from one another, and worse (Genesis 27). It was a prediction of the future of

---

1.   https://biblehub.com/psalms/28-6.htm

2.   https://biblehub.com/psalms/28-7.htm

the one over whom the father's words were spoken. It was the most precious legacy a child could receive, far above the servants and flocks and herds.

In a letter to his friends dated 6/26/03, Dr. Chuck Pierce, President of Glory of Zion Ministries in Denton, Texas. writes: "There is power in blessings. In the Bible, we bless God and God blesses us....There is power in the spoken word. Once a word is spoken, the word assumes a history of its own, almost a personality of itself... (and) has the power of its own fulfillment....The Word of God exists as a reality and has within itself the power of its own fulfillment. Formal words of blessing or cursing also have the same power of self-fulfillment."

Today, under the New Covenant created by the shed blood of Jesus the Christ, both men and women who have accepted the LORD Jesus have been made kings and priests (II Peter 2:9), "predetermined... to walk in an exalted status here on the Earth ...as we exercise authority in the Name of Jesus," according to Pastor Dan (*Divine Provision*).

With respect to the husbands being the head of their households as ordered by God (Eph. 5:23), the New Covenant empowers the Word of God—the blessing—spoken by mothers over their children to have as much impact as any their fathers would say (Galatians 3:28).

The most important thing is that the children are blessed daily, whether by father or mother, or, preferably, both, for unity is essential to the total success of the family, to the success of the covering—the spiritual protection—remaining intact. A break in the covering allows the enemy access to your kids, but through continual application of and obedience to the Word of God in our lives, that covering will be restored. As Jesus answered when He was tempted by the devil, "It is written..." (Matt. 4; Luke 4).

The Word of God is not chained, does not return empty, and accomplishes that for which it is sent by God! (Isa. 55:11)

Faith

The sky and earth (the universe, the world) will pass away, but God's Word will never pass away.—Luke 21:33, AMP

As one faithful and faith-filled Pastor is so fond of saying (to paraphrase), if you can't believe God for something big, then start believing Him for socks. *Just start!*

Believe and Speak

Faith is the first Focus Verse:

But without faith it is impossible to please *and* be satisfactory to Him. For whoever would come near to God must [necessarily] believe that God exists and that He is the rewarder of those who earnestly *and* diligently seek Him [out].- Hebrews 11:6, AMPC

Daddy God is so good! He is the God of Faith, and the Author and Finisher of our faith. Hallelujah!

2Looking away [from all that will distract] to Jesus, Who is the Leader *and* the Source of our faith [giving the first incentive for our belief] and is also its Finisher [bringing it to maturity and perfection]. He, for the joy [of obtaining the prize] that was set before Him, endured the cross, despising *and* ignoring the shame, and is now seated at the right hand of the throne of God. – Hebrews 12:2, AMPC

God speaks Faith; His language is Faith. When we speak and walk in Faith, He moves! Hallelujah!

We must believe that He loves us, and that He hears us and wants to help and reward us—just like we (imperfect) parents love and hear and want to help and reward our dear children.

As I've heard more than one minister say, "Faith is the currency of Heaven."

Actually, we all have more faith than we consciously realize; we have faith the car will start, the light

will come on when we flip on the switch, and certainly faith that the bills (and the taxes) will arrive. We have faith that the chair will hold us when we sit on it, and that the sun will appear in the morning. We have faith.

When it comes to faith in God, though, why do we waver? We can't see electricity, but we often seem to believe in it more than Him Who created it. Yet, even spiritual giants strive to have more faith.

When I was first learning about the dynamics of being a Spirit-filled Christian, I heard an associate pastor at a church in Tulsa, Oklahoma say to the crowd, "We tell the enemy, 'No, I'm not having that (curse), I'm having this (blessing of God)!'"

That marked me. I wanted that kind of faith. I wanted to be that confident knowing I could believe, proclaim, and have that which was purchased for and promised to me by the living God, the Sovereign King, Who had adopted me as His own. So how did I get it, and how did I impart it to my child?

Faith = Hearing + Action

On May 20, 2006, I sat a women's conference, listening to Teri Copeland Pearsons preach a powerful message on praying in the Spirit for wisdom. LORD, I prayed, I need more faith. Please give me more faith!

Softly came the reply. **"Faith comes by hearing and hearing by the Word of God,"** said my Father.

(Of course He would speak to me from the Word; the Book of Faith!)

But of course. How is anyone taught but that they "hear," both with their physical ears, and in their spirits, minds, and emotional experiences? It's been said that true hearing comes the moment we believe—have faith—that what we hear is true, and decide to act on that truth.

Another thing God showed me is this: "Hearing" doesn't just mean going to church to listen to the preacher. Hearing is experienced when we seek God in prayer; submit when we hear His voice; focus solely on Him in our praise, whether it's singing spiritual songs with the Christian radio station, or speaking a Psalm to Him; when we read the Word of God to ourselves and think on it. If we read it out loud, we hear the words with our physical ears.

But even when we read the Word silently, our brains, our spirits, "hear" the Word. And it builds our faith. When we give our children Bible verses to read and especially have them read them to us (which is something my little girl loves to do), they have the triple blessing of hearing them three ways. And when our darlings see us applying the Word to our lives, they "hear" yet again. Our actions flow out of what we believe. So let us live lives of faith in God!

How to Hear Better

Another important point is that hearing God's voice usually comes more frequently and easily to those who have received the baptism of the Holy Spirit (Please refer to the "First Things First" section at the front of this book.).

I can't explain it, but this miracle of empowerment from God allows believers who continue to seek Him the ability to hear and understand His voice in much greater ways; worship more deeply; experience Him in greater measure in prayer, while speaking the Word, and more!

Another thing I've learned from church is that God is always talking to us, but we're usually too busy to listen. It is a decision and a discipline to make time to be alone with God and hush our noisy souls so our spirit can hear Him speak. As Romans 10:17—which Daddy God reminded me of—says, **"Faith comes by hearing, and hearing by the Word of God."** *LORD, help us to hear and obey You today!*

Feelings Vs. Faith

One thing we must remember is that feelings and faith don't always match. Feelings cannot be trusted. According to Pastors Kenneth and Gloria Copeland, we can't get to know Jesus just through feelings, but through His Word.

We can always trust our faith in God's Word infallible Word. For He is the God that never changes—the only sublime Absolute in our volatile world (Heb. 13:8). Even if the answers aren't clear at first, we remember that He is the Answer; He loves us, and wants us to walk in wisdom, to His honor. He will help us if we are patient to wait upon Him (Psm. 33:8). He is a Spirit, and speaks to our spirits (hearts).

The worksheets for Faith follow. Get a notebook—preferably, one for yourself, and one for each child. Let the kids decorate and otherwise personalize their notebooks, with markers, stickers,, 3D items, etc., (like a cross between scrapbooking and a school binder) so that they become "treasure books," for that is indeed what they are—books of true Treasure!

You can also get notecards (especially the brightly-colored ones), and keep them for flashcard practice (like "Around the World", where two students are shown one side of a card, and the first who answers wins, and gets to go to the next student/child, to see who answers correctly first. This is most fun and effective in a group setting, for the whole group hears the question and then answer.).

Faith Exercises

As one well-known apostle stated, "The devil doesn't try us; he tries our faith."

Strong faith doesn't come overnight. Like an oak tree, our faith must have deep roots. No matter the circumstances, we must continue to know and proclaim—especially through trials—that God is good; that He that never slumbers nor sleeps; is on the throne and ever aware of every detail of our lives (Isa. 40:28); and that He is working through His Spirit (Rom. 8:28, Jer. 29:11) to show us His goodness.

Focus Verse/Faith 1:

For whatever is born of God is victorious over the world; and this is the victory that conquers the world, even our faith.—I John 5:4, AMP

To customize this verse for your child, add his or her name. I will use my daughter for the example:

"My child, you are born of God and you are victorious over the world; the victory that conquers the world is your faith." –I John 5:4, AMP

Now, please write out I John 5:4 (whatever version you want to use!) for your child(ren) and read it aloud to them. This way, both you and they are hearing and seeing it. Here is space for you and/or your children to use, and/or write it in your treasure books, or on your treasure cards, along with any insights the LORD gives you or your children.

As I told my daughter often in her school career, and especially in her 6th and 7th grades, when I homeschooled her, "Repetition's how we learn. Repetition's how we learn. Repetition's how..."

"Mommmm!" she'd say, and roll her eyes.

Another thing I liked to encourage her to do was illustrate her Scripture cards. I still have those 40 original drawings!

See how easy and interesting you can make this—for yourself and your family?

Every time you do this, you speak the life-changing Word over your children, positively shaping their destiny!

Yes, words are very powerful. They are how God created the world, and how we create our worlds, and by them, have a major impact on shaping the worlds of those under our authority.

Certain things people say to us, or how they say them, have incredible impact on our thinking. Unfortunately, most of what people remember is negative.

By speaking the Word of God and other encouragements to your child daily, you will be practicing "displacement," flushing out wrong things they've heard and filling them with spiritual, emotional, mental, social, creative, and physical confidence. You will be affecting their lives and circumstances around them in positive ways and the fruit of your efforts will appear! (Isa. 55:11)

Companion Verse/ Faith 2

"And we know (understand, recognize, are conscious of, by observation and by experience) and believe (adhere to and put faith in and rely on) the love God cherishes for us. God is love, and he who dwells and continues in love dwells and continues in God and God dwells and continues in him." —I John 4:16, AMP

Now here's the way you can write and speak it over your loved one(s) using their names:

"My child(ren), you understand and believe the love God has for you, and you dwell and continue in God Who is love, and He dwells and continues in you."—I John 4:16

It's now your turn to write I John 4:16!

One of the most powerful and wonderful aspects of our faith is knowing that God is love, and that nothing can separate us from that love (Rom. 8:31). His unending, unconditional love is the basis for everything He does! And the whole world is looking for it.

By meditating on God's perfect love for you, you will naturally and supernaturally convey this vital understanding to your little ones. And that will give them confidence like nothing else. So let's write it out now, in the treasure book(s) or treasure card(s).

Great! Be sure and read it aloud to your darlings (for faith comes by hearing, and hearing by the Word of God (Rom. 10:17)), and help them memorize Romans 8:31b to accompany it: **"If God be for us, who can be against us?"**

Write it out and say it now!

Numbers 14 tells about how the Israelites did not believe the report of Joshua and Caleb, two of the twelve spies sent to scout out the land God said He had given them. Even though there were giants there, God had given the Israelites the Promised Land, and as Joshua and Caleb knew they were "well able to possess it" through the power of God.

But most of the Israelites were doubtful. They could not believe that God wanted to pour out His blessings upon them—even though He had delivered them from the Egyptians! So God swore that none of that generation except Joshua and Caleb, who believed the LORD, would see the land flowing with the blessings of God.

As they see us live by faith and teach them the Word, our children are becoming children of great faith. And that faith pleases God. Our kids will possess the wonderful lands (destinies) that the LORD God has for them! AMEN!

The Word commends Caleb but here I will use Victoria (my favorite kid on the planet, even though, at the time of this update, she is now almost 28 and has been married almost 5 years to the covenant husband God planned for her. She's been friends with Ben many years, after meeting him at church camp!) as the example.

Companion Verse/ Faith 3

Victoria, you are like God's servant Caleb; you have a different spirit and follow God fully, so He will bring you into the land into which he has for you, and your descendants shall possess it. –Num. 14:24, AMP

I really like that verse! Since I discovered it a couple years ago, I've been quoting it over my family and myself almost daily, and of course every time I proclaim it aloud or even think it, the more it helps me forget the things of this world and follow God with all my heart (He's working on that!).

Okay, let's write and speak Numbers 14:24. You can use a journal, loose paper, notecards, your digital device, or whatever you would like.

The more I meditate on that and the many other verses I read daily (in my daily Bible reading; on my bathroom mirror; at my desk in my home office; emails to others and online reading; in the front inside covers of my books; on the Scripture cards I shared with my daughter daily; and more,) along with the Word I hear on the radio and on the CDs of Spirit-filled ministers, the more I think like Christ—the point of all of this!

It will be the same with you. The Ever-living Water of the Word will wash the wrong thinking of the world from your mind and transform your life into something beautiful, powerful, and useful to the Master (2 Tim. 2:21).

So I rejoice that you are reading this because you obviously care very deeply that your life reflects the true God, and you want to invest His best into the lives of your precious ones. HALLELUJAH!

Back to Numbers 14:24. When I found this in the Message Bible, I liked it even better, so I use this version when I speak it over my child(ren):

"LORD, your servant(s), my child(ren)...has a different spirit; he/she/they follow(s) You passionately, and You'll bring (child(ren)) into the land so that it will be inherited."—Numbers 14:24, MSG (paraphrase mine)

Till now, the verses you've seen all speak directly to child(ren), but I'm sure you noticed that I address the LORD on the child(ren)'s behalf in this one. It doesn't matter. Go with the flow of God's Spirit, and put your name, or your child's name, or your other loved one's name in the verse.

Another exciting idea is to let your precious one put your name in the Scripture, and speak it over you! That will engage and empower your child(ren) even more!

Just like in AWANA® and other Scripture-memorization programs (which I think overall are definitely beneficial!), the kids may not get it the first few times, but we help them, and it is a wonderful experience that brings glory to God! He loves to hear His Word, and when we lift Him up, He draws all men to Him! Hallelujah!

Whether I speak to my child(ren) or the LORD, the point is that His all-powerful Word is being spoken into the atmosphere of her life, shaping, leading, and inspiring them to a higher Way—His way!

Now, you and your children please write the Numbers 14:24 (Nothing wrong with writing the same Scripture twice, and the more, the better. Repetition's how we learn. Repetition's how we learn. Repetition's how... Got it? ☺)

In Mark 9:22, a man begged Jesus to heal his son of a demon, saying, **"But if You can do anything, do have pity on us and help us."**

Verse 23 is our next Companion Verse, in which the LORD once again exhorts us to have faith in Him:

Companion Verse / Faith 4

Jesus replied, "(You say to Me), If you can do anything? (Why,) all things are possible to him who believes!"—Mark 9:23, AMP

So I write it to speak over my child(ren) like this: "My child(ren), all things can be (are possible) to you who believes."—Mark 9:23, AMP

Your turn to write and speak it with your loved ones!

My daughter is anointed—gifted by God—in design. While of course I am delighted and constantly praise her every time she creates a new design, I also explain that it is Him Who gives her the ideas, that she can create anything, that there are no limits.

After all, Elohim our Creator is limitless, and endlessly creative. He lives in her, and He lives in all of us who believe. Even if your children are not yet old enough to understand and receive Christ as Savior, you can tell them every day that GOD the Creator lives in them and, as Pastor says, "God created us to create."

Now, put the names of your little creators in the Mark 9:23 verse, and read it to them. Better yet, let them read the Word out loud! Here's some space for you to do that:

For more verses on faith (they're all good!), please refer to the additional worksheets. Remember, you can never learn too many verses, and you can never have too much faith!

Remember, "Faith is the currency of Heaven." On the next page are more Scriptures for your sword.

And he said unto them, When ye pray, say, Our Father which art in heaven, Hallowed be thy name. Thy kingdom come. Thy kingdom come. Thy will be done, as in heaven, so in earth. –Luke 11:2, KJV

Faith – Additional Scriptures

And here's another jewel from an apostle who also serves as a pastor: "The gates of hell are movable barriers." One of the most effective ways to move those gates—anything coming against us that tries to keep us from drawing closer to God, or any affliction or curse from which we are freed by the Blood of Jesus (Psm. 106:10)—is to do what you are doing; learn, study, speak, and live the Word of God.

There! How's that to strengthen your faith?! Now, happy gate-moving, as you look up these Scriptures (excellent practice for you and your young ones to learn the locations of the books of the Bible, and where certain Scriptures are!). You can write them in your treasure books and/or treasure cards!

Num. 14:4 , Deut. 28:1-14
Psalm 27:1; 37:14, Psalm 91
Isa. 7:9b; 8:17
Hos. 10:12
Hab. 3:17-19
Hag. 2:4-9
Zech. 4:6,7
Mal. 3:16; 4:2,3
Matt. 13:23, 13:31, 32; 17:20
Luke 13:19; 21:33
John 11:40
Acts 4:31
Rom. 5:2; 10:8, 10:17
Eph. 1:19
Phil. 1:6; 4:13
I Tim. 6:12, II Tm 1:8
I Pet. 1:8; 2:9
I John 3:22

Use your own paper, to write out and speak these Scriptures, after you look them up (Good location practice! ☺). Record your thoughts as well.

Don't be shy about listening to God and writing what you think He is saying to you. He loves you. And, as many ministers have stated, says, God is always talking; it's just that we aren't usually listening. However, when we really want to hear the LORD, He will help us!

Then will the righteous (those who are upright and in right standing with God) shine forth like the sun in the kingdom of their Father. Let him who has ears [to hear] be listening, and let him consider and perceive and understand by hearing. – Matthew 13:43, AMPC

Worship

Not to us, O LORD, not to us but to Your name give glory, for Your mercy and lovingkindness and for the sake of Your truth and faithfulness! –Psalm 115:1, AMP

I have a photo I took at Christmas, when my daughter was six. She likes to play with Nativity scenes, and she set hers on the piano bench. On the carpet below, she posed her elegantly-dressed Southern belle, with hands raised. The doll was worshipping Jesus.

I treasure that photo. I treasured even more when Victoria (who, at the time of the first writing of this book in 2007, when she was ten) said, "Mama, let's listen to some Jesus music!" and then asked me to turn it up so she can sing along in praise to her Creator, Daddy God.

When she sang so sweetly the lines to "Amazing Grace" in that pure precious voice, I knew God was smiling, and the angels marveled. Although my darling daughter was a little shy in worship in public, her heart toward the LORD is love. She worships.

More Than Music

The worship of God often involves singing and playing of instruments, but comprises so much more.

As Darlene Zschech, the worship leader at Hillsong Church in Australia writes in her book, *Extravagant Worship*, "Worship should be a way of life, with many facets of expression."

And I'll add that true worship is not an act we perform. It is love and thanksgiving, adoration and awe for the Creator and Sustainer of life, the victorious Warrior King, the Holy One Who calls Himself Daddy God to all who will believe in Him. It flows from our hearts when we pause to wonder at His devotion (Jn. 4:24).

To paraphrase Dr. Myles Munroe in his book, *The Purpose and Power of Praise and Worship*, praise is what man does to give God glory, and worship is God's response. The LORD sees and hears and rewards us who honor Him (Heb. 11:6, Mal. 3:10, 3:16).

Why We Worship

Why do we worship? Every human worships something; it is our nature to esteem a power greater than ourselves. So why do many of us worship God?

Created To Worship

First, it is a command. We were created to worship God (Luke 4:8), and He alone is worthy (John 14:6,19:30, 20:17, Rev. 4:11, 5:12).

When we worship Him truly, we give our LORD glory by showing the angelic and demonic beings the results of our appreciation for His unconditional love (Heb. 10:1; 2 Cor. 2:14).

As a well-known minister says, "Angels do not understand grace. They go by the law."

The holy angels worship the LORD constantly and purely, and long to understand the mysteries of the New Covenant (I Pet. 1:12). As we worship, we understand more.

When we humans worship it is a choice. But personally, the closer I get to God and the more I realize all He's done for me, the more compelled I am to worship. It just flows out of my spirit—my heart. I cannot stop it. Nor do I try. And He who is worthy loves it!

The LORD says in Psalm 100:4 to "**enter His gates with thanksgiving, to enter His courts with praise praise; be thankful unto Him and bless His name.**"

Let us and/or our child(ren) write and speak Psalm 100:4.

This indicates to me that we cannot deepen that supreme relationship without a thankful heart. When we are thankful to God, we worship. And we have the power to choose to be thankful!

I do not know Hebrew, nor have I studied it. I discovered a Hebrew word, "Hiphil", which means, according to one source I found, "to flash forth light." However, what I like better is that, according to this source, in the active tense, "Hiphil" means "to cause to love."

To me, both fit our truly awesome LORD (I can only use the word "awesome" for Christ, the Father, and the Holy Trinity, for nothing else in creation is awesome, compared to them, Who are One!)!

God is Love, and God is Light!

He who does not love has not become acquainted with God [does not and never did know Him], for God is love. – I John 4:8, AMPC

And this is the message [the message of promise] which we have heard from Him and now are reporting to you: God is Light, and there is no darkness in Him at all [no, not in any way]. - I John 1:5, AMPC (and Hebrews 1:1-4).

I believe that is what happens when we worship our LORD in spirit and in truth (Rom. 12:1); our spirits shine and flash like lightning in the heavens as we sacrifice offerings of praise to the Most High, defeating the darkness and pleasing Him.

Second, we worship the LORD to drive out demonic spirits and prepare our spirits to hear and believe His holy Word to enter our hearts and build our faith (Rom. 10:17).

Since evil entered his heart and he was exiled from Heaven (Luke 10:18), the devil our enemy has been envious of God and works to steal the worship that belongs to the LORD alone (Luke 4:5-8, Matt 4:10). And he certainly comes to steal the Word if he can.

So let us worship truly, prepare, and receive the Word.

Third, we worship because it changes us; it frees and delivers and heals. God lives in our true praises (Psalm 22:3) and as we worship Him, we forget ourselves, we allow Him to create in us hearts more holy, and to expand our understanding of His greatness.

The more we worship, the more we realize our lives are not ours (I Pet. 1:18-19), and that true freedom is submitting to the wonderful, abundant, fulfilling life of the living God, called in the Greek "Zoe," or "life as God has it."

Worship is really anything you do to bring glory and honor to God; to lift Him up; to help others see the real LORD of Heaven and earth—whether it's prayer, singing, playing an instrument, parenting, gardening, cooking, cleaning, teaching, organizing, giving of your time or service or money, or anything else you do to show the love of God! Hallelujah!

He alone is worthy of our praise and worship. He alone is beautiful for every situation, every moment of life. He alone is our Help and our Shield, our High Tower, our Glory and the Lifter of our heads!

Worship Exercises

Focus Verse / Worship 1

So I have looked upon You in the sanctuary to see Your power and Your glory. Because Your loving-kindness is better than life, my lips shall praise You. So will I bless You while I live; I will lift up my hands in Your Name. –Psalm 63:2-4

So I write it for my daughter like this: "My child, you have seen the LORD in the sanctuary and beheld His power and His glory. Because His love is better than life, your lips will praise Him. You will praise Him as long as you live, and in His name you will lift up your hands."—Psalm 63:2-4

Let's go; you and your kids have this space to write (then speak) these excellent worshipful verses:

Exalting the LORD

The lifting of hands is "Yadah" or "Yodah" (Ya DAH) in Hebrew, one of the seven facets of praise14. People get excited at sports events and lift their hands and shout, and how much more should we lift our hands (Yodah) and shout to exalt the King of Glory Who gave His life for us?

We're on the winning team!

Now, it's your turn to personalize Psalm 63:2-4 for your child(ren) (Yes, even if you just wrote it. Repetition's how we learn! ☺ Practice makes better!):

Also, you may want to keep your personal daily journal handy, and, if the kids have one, that would be great for them too; you all can record insights the LORD gives you and/or your child(ren) into His Word, for He surely will!

He is the Revelation, and, when we sow His Word into our hearts, it always produces fruit (Isaiah 55:10-11)!

As humans we often exalt things that are not worthy of that honor. Only God is truly worthy to be exalted. "Exalt" means, according to the first two meanings in The Random House College Dictionary, "To elevate in rank, honor, power, character, quality, etc. 2. to praise; extol."

Praise and worship is not just found in the Psalms. It is found throughout the Bible as God deals with, delivers, blesses, and protects His people—just as He does today (Heb. 13:8). It is our privilege and honor to worship King Jesus, and why we were created!

Although He has the angels and the elders who exalt Him continuously throughout eternity (Rev. 4:9-11), He created humans with a free will. When we choose to worship, it gives Him glory greater than that He already has in Heaven!

According to Nelson's Illustrated Bible Dictionary, worship is "reverent devotion and allegiance pledged to God; the rituals or ceremonies by which this reverence is expressed."

The English word "worship" comes from the Old English word 'worthship,' a word that denotes "the worthiness of the one receiving the special honor or devotion."

Thankfully, it is possible to honor God in every part of our lives, not just when we are singing in church. God is so much bigger than the walls of the buildings where we worship and hear the preaching that I'm tempted to write several paragraphs about it. But when anyone receives the LORD Jesus as their Savior, they become a temple of God, part of His Body.

As many say, "We (believers) *are* the Church!"

Many people who call themselves believers but don't go to church have told me, "Oh I don't need to go to church; I can worship God in the woods." It's true that we can certainly worship and praise the LORD wherever we are; and we should. We are not required to perform elaborate rituals and ceremonies after fasting three days or something, just to cultivate the holy Presence of God.

The moment Jesus died, the veil that had separated us from the Holy of Holies—where the Presence

God resided—was torn. Jesus on the cross served as the Door through which the Holy One could reach out as Father to again embrace us who would call ourselves His own (Heb. 10:10-29).

So we can worship Him in the woods. Or in the kitchen. Or in the bathroom. Or in the yard. Or in the car, the bedroom, the den, at the ballgame, or anywhere else—especially with our precious kids as we speak the Word to them!

When we speak the Word with respect to Him, we exalt God. We worship.

However, we are commanded by God to gather with other believers—to go to church—and worship and receive the Word (Heb. 10:22). That is for our benefit, not God's!

Something happens when we worship and hear the Word in a corporate setting that we cannot experience on our own. We need the encouragement, prayers, and fellowship—the relationship—of others who love and follow God. When we gather with others, we can be changed from glory to glory; to continually become more like Christ, which is why we are on the planet!

And all of us, as with unveiled face, [because we] continued to behold [in the Word of God] as in a mirror the glory of the Lord, are constantly being transfigured into His very own image in ever increasing splendor and from one degree of glory to another; [for this comes] from the Lord [Who is] the Spirit. – 2 Corinthians 3:18, AMPC

The enemy through people who don't respect and even state they hate God (which baffles me, for our merciful, gracious, faithful, and patient God is the reason we all have breath and any and every good thing!) has attempted to stifle our liberty in some public places, but we always have the freedom to worship in our hearts and minds. No being can take that away from us!

We also can rejoice that we truly have the right and freedom in the USA, to worship the true Christ, the LORD Jesus, the only Savior of the world, anytime, anywhere, and in various ways—with God-honoring respect to others, of course. That freedom to honor God is increasing with the right leadership! Hallelujah!

Through true worship, the presence of God is manifested, our souls are washed and transformed, and through worship, spiritual battles are won. LORD, teach us to worship You! Through worship, we are transformed into more of His image, which is the true goal of our lives! Companion Verse 2 is next.

Companion Verse/ Worship 2

I bow before Your holy Temple as I worship. I praise Your name for Your unfailing love and faithfulness; for Your promises are backed by all the honor of Your name.—Psalm 138:2, NLT

My example: "My child, you bow before God as you worship in His temple. You praise His name for His unfailing love and faithfulness to you; He promises are secure in His holy Name." –Psalm 138:2

Your turn.

By the way, I have found it very beneficial—every day of my life!—to keep worship music or true Biblical preaching and teaching playing in the background during these times. I actually work and create very well (as I'm doing right now, as I write!), with anointed teaching of the Word off the internet playing. The LORD can help us do this—understand and listen to the Word, even as we are using (at least some of) that same part of our brains to put words on paper. Hallelujah!

One reason for that is because the Presence—the Spirit—of the LORD inhabits His praise—whether it is true Bible-based preaching and teaching, or true Bible-based worship. Hallelujah!

Some people keep Bible-based preaching and teaching or worship playing in the background 24/7, at least in one room of the house. This is always going to be beneficial, for the atmosphere of your home can determine the success of your lives, and the atmosphere of your home, of your family, is mostly determined by what's going on spiritually—to the glory of the LORD Jesus Christ, or not.

By the way, when our hearts are tuned to God, we are more aware of His Presence; more thankful for His goodness; more inspired and inclined to walk in love, and thus to be better examples of the true Christ to others, especially to our families!

As Dr. Chuck Pierce says in his book, *The Worship Warrior*, "Individual worship brings transformation."

One excellent way to worship is to proclaim the Scriptures out loud, as we've discussed throughout this book. The purpose of worship is to change us to be like Jesus, as we exalt the LORD and enjoy Him.

This brings us to Companion Verse 3.

Companion Verse/ Worship 3

Praise the LORD, O my soul; all my inmost being, praise his holy name. Praise the LORD, O my soul, and forget not all his benefits; who forgives all your sins and heals all your diseases, who redeems your life from the pit and crowns you with love and compassion, who satisfies your desires with good things so that your youth is renewed like the eagle's.—Psalm 103:1-5

Here's how I write it: "My child(ren), you praise the LORD with all your soul; you praise His holy name and remember all His benefits; He has forgiven your sins, healed your diseases, redeemed your life from the pit and crowned you with love and compassion, and satisfied your desire with good things." –Psalm 103:1-5

Time for you to do so!

It is hard to pick a favorite chapter, not to mention verse, in God's awesome Word. Here is one of my favorites:

Companion Verse / Worship 4

I will bless the LORD at all times; His praise shall continually be in my mouth. My life makes its boast in the LORD; let the humble and afflicted hear and be glad. O magnify the LORD with me and let us exalt His name together. I sought (inquired of) the

Lord and required Him [of necessity and on the authority of His Word], and He heard me, and delivered me from all my fears.–Psalm 34:1-4, AMP

Here's how I like to customize it for my daughter (and others): "(My child(ren), you bless the LORD at all times; His praise is always in your mouth. You boast in the LORD, and that makes discouraged people glad. You join in the praise of others who love and exalt Him. When you are afraid, you seek Him, and He delivers you and gives you peace."—Psalm 34:1-4, AMP

So go for it.

On the next page, I've listed additional verses for you. If they don't seem to be about worship to you, pause to ask the LORD to speak to you about them.

Enjoy! Remember, even as you study, even as you write and pray and proclaim, you are worshipping God.

Worship – Additional Scriptures

Precious child(ren) You give glory to the Name of the LORD, for His mercy and lovingkindness, for His truth and faithfulness to you.—Psalm 115:1

Your turn! Here's another jewel for the sword:

Therefore You are great, O Lord God; for none is like You, nor is there any God besides You, according to all [You have made] our ears to hear.—2 Sam. 7:22, NIV

Now you write it, and/or have your child(ren) write it.

It's hard to "stop" listing the wonderful Word of God, but my intent is to lead you into choosing additional verses for yourself and your sweet child(ren). Allow me to get you started, though! :-)

My darling(s), you give glory to the Name of the LORD, for His mercy and lovingkindness, for His truth and faithfulness to you.—Psalm 115:1

Now, you go! Here are other verse references for you.

2 Sam. 7:22

Psalm 66:1-2, 67:3, 68:3, 75:1, 84:11-12, 90:1-2, 98:1, 99:1-3, 104:1-2, 106:1, 108:1, 111:1, 112:1

Here are more Scriptures for you to consider:

Ex. 23:21-23

Josh. 24:15

I Sam. 2:1-3

Job. 42:2

Psalm. 44:6-8; 50:23; 119:89

Prov. 10:11, 20, 21

Ecc. 9:10

Isa. 55:2

Hos. 10:12

Luke 1:46-49

John. 4:34; 9:4

Rom. 12:1,2; 15:17

I Thes. 5:21

2 Tim. 2:21

Now write out these verses. (Don't be pressured or overwhelmed; you don't have to do them all today! You can just do one a day, if that's what the LORD is leading you to do for your family. God is a Leader, not a driver!), and your thoughts as you want.

Remember, when you read the Word, write the Word, speak the Word, and especially when you live the Word, you are worshipping (Mal. 3:16, John 4:23-24). So write and speak!

Remember, too, that God does not expect us to have perfect voices. He tells us to simply, "Make a joyful noise"—and He tells us that several times in Psalms (66:1, 81:1, 95:1 and 2, 98:4 and 6, and 100:1), as if reassuring us that it doesn't matter whether we are singing, playing the piano, banging on drums or a banana tree, clinking a spoon against a glass, or shouting His Word at the top of our lungs.

As long as what we do is led by the Spirit and is in order so as to not disturb the service in any ungodly way; as long as our worship, however we express it, is coming from our hearts to shower Him with praise and adoration and thanksgiving, He accepts it as worship. Praise God!

For more examples on how to worship, study what worshippers of today and years past do! Some that have really shaped my life are Carman, Dave Crowder, Chris Thomlin, Mercy Me, Elevation Worship, Jesus Culture, Worship Mob, Steven Curtis Chapman, Darlene Zschech of Hillsong, Matt Redman, Chris Tomlin, Mary Alessi, John Tesh, Among Thorns, Danny Chambers, Danny Goke, Vicki Yohe, Big Daddy Weave, King and Country, Lauren Daigle, and several more.

True worship will always change you, when you engage your heart and soul (mind, will emotions)!

The LORD will lead you to those true worshipers who will inspire you the most.

Through worship, the presence of God is manifested, and through worship, spiritual battles are won.

23 But a time is coming and has now come when the true worshipers will worship the Father in spirit and in truth, for the Father is seeking such as these to worship Him. 24 God is Spirit, and His worshipers must worship Him in spirit and in truth."—John 4:23-24, Berean Standard Bible

LORD, teach us to worship You!

Wisdom

"Your Word is a lamp to my feet and a light to my path."—Psalm 119:105

Write then speak (with your young ones) Psalm 119:105 now:

It is only by truth—the wisdom of God's Word—that we know how to successfully operate in and conquer this world as co-laborers with Christ the King.

The days are evil, the land filled with dragons who seek to devour our children (Jer. 10:22, Rev. 12:1-4). We must have God's mind to rise and occupy (Luke 19:13), take this earth for Him Who rightly owns it (Jer. 10:12), and train our children to do the same.

Until the LORD returns to make things right (Jer. 10:10, Rev. 22:3, 7, 12, 13), we have work to do (John 9:4)!

Highest Wisdom

Instructing our children in the things of God is the highest wisdom. God says in Proverbs 4:5-6, AMP to **"Get skillful and Godly wisdom, get understanding (discernment, comprehension, and interpretation); do not forget and do not turn back from the words of my mouth. Forsake not (Wisdom) and she will keep, defend, and protect you; love her and she will guard you."**

Let's do it; write and speak Proverbs 4:5-6 for your kid(s) and yourself!

The more we dig into God's Word and apply it to our lives, the wiser we will be, and not only will we consciously, purposely training them in Zoe life, but subconsciously; as we walk with Him, so will our children see our example and be highly inclined to follow.

The following pages include selected verses to speak to and about them to help them walk in the wisdom of God.

Wisdom Exercises

In Deuteronomy 5, Moses called the people of Israel together to remind them of the commandments of the LORD. He reiterated the Ten Commandments. Then in verses 32 and 33, he told them that they must fully follow all of God's ways:

Focus Verse / Wisdom 1

"Therefore you people shall be watchful to do as the LORD your God has commanded you; you shall not turn aside to the right hand or to the left. You shall walk in all the ways which the LORD your God has commanded you, that you may live and that it may go well with you and that you may live long in the land which you shall possess."—Deut. 5:32-33, AMP

So I write it for my darling daughter like this: "My child, you are careful to do what the LORD your God has commanded you, in every way. You walk in all the ways of the LORD God, and you live long and prosper and prolong your days in the land you possess."—Deut. 5:32-33, AMP

Now write it out for your kids (and, as you've already deduced, when they ask what a certain word means, you stop and explain it to them, and/or help them look it up in the dictionary. So, that's another reason you may just want to focus on one or two verses a day or session!)

You Are Free to Ask for Help

If you feel you need more wisdom, ask God; He is glad to help us be wise (James 1:5)!

Once, when I actually prayed and asked Him to help direct me on what I considered a very small matter, He told me, "I'll always help you if you will just ask Me."

He cares so much He gave Jesus for us! So take advantage of the mercy and grace He extends to you through the Blood Covenant of Christ (Heb. 13:20), and ask for help. As our Father, God is approachable anytime, anywhere, about anything (Heb. 4:16, 13:6), when there is no conscious unconfessed sin in our lives hindering that relationship.

As caring parents, we are vigilant to watch over our little ones to protect them from harm. One of the best ways to do that, of course, is what you're doing—speaking the Truth—the Word of God—over and about them daily, and often during the day.

Praise the LORD, He Who never grows weary is ever watching and continuously teaching our human hearts to stay on the Path.

He is forever faithful!

Knowing God Means Honoring Him

Praise God we are made righteous in His sight (only) by the Blood of Jesus that covers us (I Cor. 1:30),

not by what we do or don't do (Eph. 2:9). But our rewards are based on how we follow God's Word (I Cor. 3:8, Rev. 22:12), and this involves much about cleansing and keeping ourselves from evil.

"Evil" means anything that offends God. To understand what offends Him, we have to know Him intimately. Just as we know what bothers our mates, our children, our closest friends because we know their ways and how we think, how much more should we want and work to know what pleases and offends the One Who gave all for us?

As you spend more time in His Word, you will hear His voice more quickly and easily. The Holy Spirit has checked me more than once on things, by strong and frequent impressions, or sometimes His voice speaking to my mind and heart that something offended Him. And these things He showed me that offended Him were things that many other Christians "didn't see anything wrong with."

I don't care about what other Christians think if I know that I know that God is telling me to separate myself from something or someone in my life; no one but me will stand before God and answer for what I've done. And no one else will be standing with you.

Neither you nor anyone else are going to be with your darling child(ren) when they stand before the LORD. So by teaching them to love the Word, to hear and obey God, and they will be rewarded for a righteous life. It is wisdom to honor Him.

Love Rules

The first part of the upcoming verse, Romans 12:9, is about love. As I John 4:16 says, God (Who is Wisdom) is Love. As many Spirit-filled pastors have stated, "We must stay in the love walk, or our faith won't work (I Cor. chapter 13, AMP).

If our faith doesn't work, we will not fulfill our destinies and will often be frustrated.

So it is wisdom to walk in faith by sincere (unconditional) love (Gal. 5:6). We prove our love for God by obeying Him (I Jn. 14:21).

God is holy, and we must continually ask if there is anything or anyone in our lives that offends Him—then be willing to sever those ties, activities, and/or habits that He reveals are harmful to us. What we allow in our homes, in our lives, our little ones will think is all right.

The enemy is forever trying to persuade us that "a little (sin) won't hurt."

So who are you going to believe—God Who loves you, or the deceiver who wants to destroy you and your babies as quickly as possible?

Companion Verse/ Wisdom 2

(Let your) love be sincere (a real thing); hate what is evil (loathe all ungodliness; turn in horror

from wickedness), but hold fast to that which is good. –Rom. 12:9, AMP

Following is the way I write it: "My dear daughter, your love is sincere (a real thing); you hate what is evil (loathe all ungodliness, turn in horror from wickedness), but hold fast to that which is good."—Rom. 12:9, AMP

Now, your turn to write and speak Romans 12:9.

It is also wisdom to use this very short time we have wearing these "earth-suits" (James 4:14) to use all we have (skills, talents, money, material possessions, relationships, opportunities, etc.) to help advance the Kingdom.

As I've told my child(ren), and myself, my spouse, and many others through the years, we are here for many reasons; not just to have a good time.

In fulfilling God's plan for our lives, we are deeply satisfied. This brings me to the next verse:

Companion Verse / Wisdom 3

So it is with yourselves; since you are so eager and ambitious to possess spiritual endowments and manifestations of the (Holy) Spirit, (concentrate on) striving to excel and to abound (in them) in ways that will build up the church. –I Cor. 14:12

And here's how I speak it over my child: "Precious, you are eager and ambitious to possess spiritual endowments and manifestations of the (Holy) Spirit, (concentrating on) striving to excel and abound (in them) in ways that will build up the church."—I Cor. 14:12, AMP

Your children have many gifts that God has given them for His glory. Ask Him to show you how to

help your children fully develop them. He will!

Now, write out I Cor. 14:12 for them, or let them write them, or both, then speak them; together is a great way, or the echo effect:

Another part of wisdom besides daily speaking the Word of God is guarding our tongues so that the other words we speak please the LORD and benefit all who hear them (Prov. 15:23).

If you or others close to your kids have had a habit of saying negative things about them, know that those wrong words are damaging your children! Your kids are in enough battles dealing with the enemy and the world without wrong words discouraging and stifling and hindering them.

The enemy can literally set up spiritual strongholds (which I call "wrongholds"!) to harm your children's spirits and minds because of wrong words! As one pastor said, "Words are containers. They contain life or death," (Prov. 18:20, 21; Jam. 1:19). So speak life!

Our goal is not only to make our children stronger in the battle of this life, but victorious. The words you speak to and over them, and the words they speak about themselves have an incredible impact on their victory.

The more you feed yourself and your children with the nourishing fruit of the Word, the more they speak the right things because their minds and hearts are full of the everlasting, life-giving, victory-bringing Word of God (Rom. 12:2)!

Companion Verse / Wisdom 4

From the fruit of his words a man shall be satisfied with good, and the work of a man's hands shall come back to him (as a harvest).—Prov. 12:14

Here's how I write it: "My child, you speak words that bear good fruit, and the work of your hands gives you a good harvest.—Prov. 12:14.

Now, you guys do it:

Additional Scriptures and worksheets follow. Meanwhile, write your thoughts, and/or those of your child(ren), in the space below, and/or in your own treasure notebooks or treasure cards.

This *Legacy* workbook will become (as mine is, with my daughter's 6 and 7 grade writing; she is now 27, and has been married 4 years, to her best friend of 12 years! God is so faithful!) a treasured keepsake for you and your child(ren), not to mention a book of beloved Scriptures that have been changing your life and your loved ones' lives!

Now, please write your favorite Bible verses, and your thoughts, and even draw pictures yourself (or let your child(ren) do any and all of that!).

Wisdom – Additional Scriptures

All of these Scriptures would be excellent to speak over and about your children.

I have left space for you under each one to write them out with your kid(s)' names. However, if your kids are old enough, it would be even better to lead them to write the verses themselves!

Remember, you can speak the Word any time of day or night, anywhere, about your children, and it will affect their lives for God. The Word has dynamite power, called "dunamis" in Hebrew.

It will not return empty but accomplish that for which God is pleased and has purposed to send it through your mouth into the future of your kids (Isa. 55:11, AMP).

So let's get started! Some of these will include my daughter's name. Just replace it with the name of your precious one(s).

Here's how I do it: **"(Child)ren, you walk with the wise and are becoming wise."** –Prov. 13:20a

Your turn.

Psalm 26:4-8, 11-12 is a series of verses written by King David. Teach your children to quote them as a passage or separately:

4 I do not sit with false persons, nor fellowship with pretenders;

5 I hate the company of evildoers and will not sit with the wicked.

6 I will wash my hands in innocence, and go about Your altar, O Lord,

7 That I may make the voice of thanksgiving heard and may tell of all Your wondrous works.

8 Lord, I love the habitation of Your house, and the place where Your glory dwells.

11 But as for me, I will walk in my integrity; redeem me and be merciful and gracious to me.

12 My foot stands on an even place; in the congregations will I bless the Lord.

Remember to let your child(ren) illustrate the verses, and you may want to do that too! So go for it now; write then speak it, and remember to let your kids speak the Word, as often as possible! If they haven't already, they'll soon be volunteering to say The Word out loud, and oh, what music to God's ears (and yours!).

When teaching Scriptures, you and your children need to learn them just as they are written in any trusted Bible translated from the original languages of Hebrew (Old Testament) and Greek (New Testament). However, it is fine to condense the verse a bit, as I have sometimes, as long as the meaning is not changed.

The meaning of the verse is what you want to proclaim over your child, and plant deep within that little heart. Water it with more and more of the Word (John 4:10, 11), and it will bear fruit!

My child(ren), you do not make friends with those who lie or do evil, but you draw close to the LORD, and you thank Him often and brag on His wonderful deeds. You love to worship in His house. You walk in integrity and the LORD redeems you and is merciful and gracious to you. You are stable in the LORD and you bless Him in public. --Psalm 26:4-8, 11-12

Yes, let's do it again! (Even if you and your kid(s) don't write it again, you can at least say it again! Repetition's how we learn...!)

Here are more great Scriptures to write and speak:

You, my child(ren), **seek to please God and not men.** —Gal.1:10

My child(ren), **you are becoming holy because God is holy.** —I Peter 1:16

God's covenant with you, my child(ren), is to give you life and peace because of the (reverent and worshipful) fear with which (you, His priest) revere His Name and stand in awe of His Name. —Malachi 2:46

My child(ren), **the LORD sees the heart in your honor (of Him).**—Malachi 3:10

My child(ren), **you abhor what is evil and cling to what is good.**—Rom. 12:9b

You, precious one(s), **keep yourself pure and unspotted from the world.** - James 1:27

My child(ren), **you prepare your mind for action; you are self-controlled; you set your hope fully on the grace to be given you when Jesus Christ is revealed.** —I Pet. 1:13, NIV

You, dear kid(s), **listen to God and eat what is good, and your soul(s) delights itself in fatness (spiritual abundance).**—Isaiah 55:2

My child(ren), **you are of God because you listen to God.** —John 8:47

My child(ren), **God is your Father and you love Jesus, and respect and welcome Him greatly.** –John 8:42

You, dear children, **are from God and have overcome them, because the One Who is in you is greater than the one who is in the world.** –I John 4:4

You, my sweetheart(s) **keep your heart with all diligence, for out of it are the issues of life.** –Prov. 4:23

You, my dear child(ren), **are a wise child and you bring great joy to your Father in Heaven and to all of us who love and lead you.** –Prov. 10:1

Lord, You will bless My child(ren), who does not compromise her integrity; she is upright and in right standing with You; as with a shield You will surround her with goodwill (pleasure and favor). – Psalm 5:12, AMP

(It is fine to address the LORD on behalf of your child, or to address your child directly. What matters is being sensitive to the leading of the Holy Spirit.)

Now, you write and speak them.

You, darling(s), **do what is right (what you are called to do) and you prosper.** –II Chron. 31:20-21

Blessed are you, my child(ren), because you have ears to hear (the LORD) and you listen and understand.—Mark 4:23

Glory to God, my child(ren), **you hear the Word and grasp and comprehend it; you bear (spiritual) fruit and yield in one case a hundred times, in another sixty times as much was sown, in another thirty.**—Matt. 13:23

My child(ren), **the God of our LORD Jesus Christ, the Father, grants you the spirit of wisdom and revelation (of insight into mysteries and secrets) in the deep knowledge of Him.** –Eph. 1:17

My child(ren), **you do not fear, for the LORD is with you; He is your God. He strengthens you and helps you; He upholds you with His righteous right hand.** –Isa. 41:10

I have no greater joy than to know that you, my child(ren), are living your life in the Truth.—3 John 1:4

The Spirit of Truth abides in You, My child(ren), and teaches you all things. He causes you to remember all I have told you.—John 14:26

My child(ren), **you keep the commandments of the Lord your God, to walk in His ways and [reverently] fear Him.**—Deut. 8:6, AMP

My precious child(ren), **The LORD has given you the capacity to hear and obey His law, and He desires that more than sacrifice.** —Psalm 40:6

You, precious daughter(s) **have the inward adorning and beauty of the hidden person of the heart, with the incorruptible and unfading charm of a gentle and peaceful spirit, (which is not anxious or wrought up, but) is very precious in the sight of God.**—Peter 3:4

My dynamite child(ren), **you are worthy of respect and serious, not a gossiper, but temperate and self-controlled, [thoroughly] trustworthy in all things.** –I Tim. 3:11

Your mouth(s), my dear child(ren), speaks excellent and princely things, and you speak right things. Wrongdoing is loathsome and detestable to your lips. Your mouth utters truth. All the words of your mouth are righteous (upright and in right standing with God); there is nothing contrary to truth or crooked in them. –Prov. 5:6-8

My child(ren), (you) **²Do not be conformed to this world (this age), [fashioned after and adapted to its external, superficial customs], but be transformed (changed) by the [entire] renewal of your mind [by its new ideals and its new attitude], so that you may prove [for yourselves] what is the good and acceptable and perfect will of God, even the thing which is good and acceptable and perfect [in His sight for you].** – Romans 12:2, AMPC

You dwell in the secret place of the Most High and remain stable and fixed under the shadow of the Almighty [Whose power no foe can withstand]. You say of the Lord, "He is my Refuge and my Fortress, my God; on Him I lean and rely, and in Him I [confidently] trust!" For He will deliver you from the snare of the fowler and from the deadly pestilence. He will cover you with His pinions, and under His wings shall you trust and find refuge; His truth and His faithfulness are a shield and a buckler. —Psalm 91:1-4 AMP

You and all my spiritual children are disciples taught by the LORD and obedient to His will, and great is your peace and undisturbed composure (because you are obedient). –Isa. 54:13, AMP

Dear Child(ren), the Book of God's Law does not depart out of your mouth, but you are careful to do all that is written in it, and

He makes your way prosperous and successful. The God of Heaven gives you success.—Josh. 1:8, Neh. 2:20

One of the things that blesses me is that, every time I say my daughter's name (Victoria Dawn), I am really saying, "Victory"!

Names are so important; exciting stuff! But even more important is the words you speak daily over your child(ren) and other loved ones.

Just think—every time you write and especially speak the Word of God to and about your child(ren), you are changing their lives (and yours!) for good—because you're changing their lives for God! HALLELUJAH!

I've listed the references for many more Scriptures, and there are lines and other space to write them on, along with other insights God may give you.

You'll discover that your Heavenly Father will also give you insight as you write out your thoughts and prayers to Him. Remember, when you read His Word, you are reading His love letter to you. You are communicating with Jesus. He loves you.

Enjoy the process as you sharpen your sword and defend your little ones, who are made more victorious every time the Word works in their lives!

Everything you and your children need is in God's Book, the Holy Bible.

Remember, too, that it is ultimately Jehovah Sabaoth, the LORD of Armies, the LORD of Hosts, Jesus the King, the SAVIOR, DELIVERER, PRESERVER; PROTECTOR, PROVIDER, CONQUERER, SPIRIT GUIDE) Who is our Victorious Warrior—and He has already won!

Hallelujah! Blessed be the LORD, for He is good; for His mercy endures forever!

Here are more excellent Scriptures for you to enjoy. Don't worry; no pressure! You can pick and choose. You can even close your eyes and point, and know the LORD your Daddy God is so good that He will guide you! He can work with anything, any time, anywhere, to help you! Hallelujah!

Remember, He takes great delight in you, His precious child (no matter how old you are, for when you believe in Christ Jesus as Savior and LORD, you are His kid!), and loves it when you turn your heart to His Word (His Love Letter to us all; the ultimate Success Manual for a Wonderful Life!), which is, praise Him, eternal, unchanging, and always full of life! Hallelujah!

Old Testament:

Deut. 5:32, 33; 6:5-7; 7:6

I Kings 2:9 and 4:29

Psalm 16:3, 17:3; 18:21; 37:30,31; 38:37; 51:10, 119:30-32

Prov. 1:33, 3:9-10, 4:1, 10:4b, 10:13a, 10:17, 10:20a, 11:18, 11:30, 12:1, 12:8, 12:14, 13:9, 13:13, 13:18, 13:20

Isa. 54:13

Jer. 15: 16

Hos. 10:12

New Testament:

Matt. 13:16

Mark 4:24

Luke 21:19; 24:45

John 6:63, 8:31, 32, 47

Acts 13:46

I Cor. 2:12

2 Cor. 7:4, 10:3-5

Eph. 1:17, 1:19

Phil. 3:3; 4:9

Col.1:9

Heb.11:11

I Thes. 2:4, 11-13

I Pet. 1:8

Jude 20-25

And there's MORE!

Enjoy the journey in the Word, as you look up these verses with your family, and speak them. Remember to record your thoughts, and those of your little one(s). This will make a great heirloom!

Destiny

"Get up! Cry out at night, every hour on the hour. Pour your heart out like water in the presence of the LORD. Lift up your hand to Him (in prayer) for the life of your little children who faint from (spiritual) hunger at every street corner." —Lamentations 2:19, God's Word Translation

Right; time to write and speak Lamentations 2:19!

The following story is about destiny. (It is somewhat graphic, but a natural picture of very negative things that can happen in the spirit, if things are not right with God!)

John and Ann were expecting. When Ann was still pregnant, she told John she was a little nervous about the cold-blooded pets he kept, some in the house. He laughed and told her not to worry.

The baby came, bright, and beautiful, innocent and pure. After their daughter was born, Ann again expressed her concern over the snakes John kept as pets. John considered himself a loving parent, but he liked those snakes, and besides, the sales he made from them helped pay the bills. So again, he told her not to worry, and Ann complied.

Soon, the little one didn't need to be nursed anymore and was sleeping soundly in her own room. John and Ann enjoyed more restful nights. Then one night, Ann awoke suddenly and, although she hadn't heard her baby cry, she decided to check on her darling.

She moved close to the bed and peeped over, straining her eyes in the dim light to gaze at her beautiful little girl.

Nothing could describe her horror as she saw the boa constrictor, dark and huge, in the bed. It had just finished eating her child!

Destiny On Purpose

You might wonder why I started this chapter about Destiny on such a morbid note. Here's why: Unless you purposely point your child to Christ as soon as possible, and keep reinforcing Godly principles by living for the LORD—both by attending a church that preaches the full Word and by reading it daily; adore Christ and worship Him; not adoring the things of the world more than His presence.

You can also ask God what may be in your home, and what relationships may be in your live(s) that offend Him, then obey Him when He shows you what to sever and destroy; watch and pray for your children to shun evil, draw close to God and follow Him all their days; and continue to love and learn God's Word and teach His instructions to your children, your kids could easily become prey to the enemy—easily!

Ask me how I know. But God is forever faithful, and far greater is King Jesus in us, than the enemy who is defeated in the world (I John 3:8 and 4:4)!

There are exceptions, but it's almost guaranteed your children won't follow God with all their hearts if you don't, unless He in His mercy sends others across their paths to teach them His ways, and the Holy Spirit draws them to respond. But responsibility for spiritual training in battle starts at home, the fortress where the Captain of our Salvation has placed the young recruits called your kids.

And we are in a battle, remember? However, this battle is one that, if we allow Christ to do these things through us, is already won!

John Hagee, in Seven Secrets of Success, says, "One can never go wrong praying Scripture over one's child. It helps unlock their God-given destiny."

Your children might have great success financially and socially, perhaps even stardom, but what about the future of their souls?

As Matthew 16:26 and 27 say, **"What does it profit a man if he shall gain the whole world, and lose his own soul? Or what shall a man give in exchange for his soul? For the Son of man (King Jesus) shall come in the glory of His Father with His angels; and then He shall reward every man according to his works."** (emphasis of "King Jesus" mine)

On the measuring tape of eternity, as a well-known minister says, our lives are less than a pinpoint (Psalm 90:5, 6 and James 4:14). There are no atheists nor agnostics standing at the edge of hell. They die and understand *God is*, and *is The LORD*.

Good Dream vs. God Dream

But it is not too late for your kids. Forget the "American Dream." The life that you seek for your children is Zoe, the Greek word for "abundant life," or "life as God has it." Investing in the proper spiritual heritage of your children—true success—will bring rewards that far outlast those of worldly gain.

So which do you want for your precious little ones? Your answer will have a major influence on their destiny. Your goals determine your motives, which can be surprisingly skewed and cloaked as "the best for the children," when they are not.

As we strive to live to the glory of God we must ask ourselves these questions, and often. Even as I write, the Holy Spirit is showing me that there is more that I can do to help bring my daughter closer to Him. And, He is also showing me, in His magnificent way, that I can't do this alone. Nor do I have to. None of us do; we depend on God to help us and He does. Hallelujah.

Having been a believing single mother for almost seven years; having overcome divorce and many other setbacks; finally triumphing in understanding (with thanks to the many ministers I've listened to through the years, that have taught me the truth of God's Word!) that I am righteous by the blood of Jesus that covers me (II Cor. 5:21); and also—miracle of miracles—thankfully receiving and marrying Clayton, the man that God meant to help complete my destiny, I have proven God's Word. It works!

Heavenly Help

God is alive; He is everywhere and will never leave those who have received and follow Him!

God is faithful; how many times have you had just what you needed when you needed it, and often in the most delightful, surprising way?

God is good!

God is The King, our loving Abba Father Who created and sustains heaven and earth and all that lives, cares about every detail of our lives, and wants to be involved. So invite Him in. You'll never regret it!

He wants to help us train and love and bless the child(ren) He has so graciously given us for a season—to know Him, to love Him, to comprehend their glorious identity in Christ, and to serve in His holy presence. Rejoice, be glad! As Jesus said on the cross, It is finished! (John 19:30)

The war is already won, and if you are born again in Jesus, you are on the winning team! (Rom. 8:37)

By doing what Jesus would do (in fact, what He desires to do through you!), you're already taking steps to empower your children them to live deeper, stronger, fuller and freer in the LORD.

Know this: As I Corinthians 15:58 says, **"...be steadfast, immovable, always abounding in the work of the LORD, for you know that your labor in the LORD is not in vain!"** HALLELUJAH!

Now, record your Scriptures and thoughts, and have your child(ren) do the same.

Destiny Exercises

Focus Verse / Destiny 1

The secret [of the sweet, satisfying companionship] of the Lord have they who fear (revere and worship) Him, and He will show them His covenant and reveal to them its [deep, inner] meaning. –Psalm 25:14, AMP

Here's how I write this glorious truth to proclaim over my daughter:

My child, you have the secret of the sweet, satisfying companionship of the LORD because you revere and worship Him, and He shows you His covenant and reveals to you its meaning.—Psalm 25:14

Now please personalize this to start proclaiming it for your children (even adults!)

Companion Verse / Destiny 2

He has lifted up a horn for His people [giving them power, prosperity, dignity, and preeminence], a song of praise for all His godly ones, for the people of Israel, who are near to Him. Praise the Lord! (Hallelujah!)—Psalm 148:14, AMP

One thing I want you to note is that the LORD is not just talking about people of Jewish heritage here.

No, "the people of Israel, who are near to Him," includes every one of us who have faith in the LORD Jesus Christ and have received Him as our Savior. We Gentiles who believe are His people too (Matt 12:21, Rom. 11:11). HALLELUJAH!

Here is how I write this for my child: My darling, the LORD has lifted up a horn for you, one of His people, giving you power, prosperity, dignity, and preeminence, a song of praise for all His godly ones, for the people of Israel, who are near to Him. Praise the LORD! Hallelujah!

Now please write this verse, and personalize it for your precious one(s):

It feels good to dig in and make God's Word personal, doesn't it? And the glory of it can only be measured in Heaven.

COMPANION VERSE / Destiny 3 **Who were chosen and foreknown by God the Father and consecrated (sanctified, made holy) by the Spirit to be obedient to Jesus Christ (the Messiah) and to be sprinkled with [His] blood: May grace (spiritual blessing) and peace be given you in increasing abundance [that spiritual peace to be realized in and through Christ, freedom from fears, agitating passions, and moral conflicts].** —Peter 1:2, AMP

This is the way I do it: My Darling Dynamite Daughter, you were chosen and foreknown by God and consecrated by the Spirit to be obedient to Jesus Christ: Grace and peace (freedom from fears, wrong passions, and moral conflicts) is given to you in increasing abundance.

Now, please write it out for your darlings.

Companion Verse/ Destiny 4

Rather, let our lives lovingly express truth [in all things, speaking truly, dealing truly, living truly]. Enfolded in love, let us grow up in every way and in all things into Him Who is the Head, [even] Christ (the Messiah, the Anointed One. —Eph. 4:15, AMP

My little one(s), your life lovingly expresses truth in all things. Enfolded in God's love, you are growing up in every way and in all things into Christ the Anointed One.—-Eph. 4:15, AMP

Now, your turn.

There! You've done it. You have now customized more extremely powerful Scriptures to proclaim over your child(ren).

Good For You!

As I said at the beginning of this book, it was hard to choose because (all together now!): "It's all good!" So these next few are additional Scriptures I feel would be good to proclaim over your darlings.

But it's *your* work and *your* and your children, so if you just want to dig into your Bible and choose those verses that otherwise appeal to you, great. Go ahead, feast!

Destiny – Additional Scriptures

By now, you know the pattern, so I'm just going to write these as I would speak them over my child, then you can write them for your precious darlings.

You are of God, little child(ren), and have overcome them, because greater is He that is in you, than he that is in the world.—John 4:4

Child(ren), as for you and your house, you will serve the LORD.—Josh 24:15

Supernatural signs follow you because you are a believer. You read your Bible, pray, and follow God's direction...and God moves in your life.—Es. 14:15-16, Jud. 16-17, Rom. 9

You, child(ren), are like a tree firmly planted (and tended) by the streams of water, and you bring forth fruit in your season; everything you do shall prosper and come to maturity. –Psalm 1:3

Child(ren), you open your lips and declare God's praise.—Psalm 51:15

The Word of God that goes forth out of His mouth through yours, my dear child(ren), shall accomplish that which He pleases and purposes, for which He sent it. –Isa. 55:1011

Darling child(ren), you know that the LORD has chosen you to loose the chains of injustice and untie the cords of the yoke, to set the oppressed free, and break every yoke.—Isa. 58:6

Precious, you are uncompromisingly righteous and your mouth utters wisdom and your tongue speaks with justice. –Psalm 38:30

You, child(ren), forget the past and strain to reach those marvelous things that are before you. You press toward the mark God has sent you toward. —Phil. 3:13

By little and little the LORD is driving out from before you all your enemies, and you are increasing and inheriting the land, my dear child(ren).—Ex. 23:30

Precious one(s), you are Christ's ambassador, and God is making His appeal through you. –John 7:16, AMP

Child(ren), you are far from even the thought of oppression, and you stand fast in the liberty (freedom) in which Christ has made you free!—Gal. 5:1 and 2 Tim. 1:17

Child(ren), you thirst for the LORD and go to Him and drink; You believe on Him and out of your belly flows rivers of living water. —John 7:38

You are sent by God, child(ren), and beautiful are the feet of you who brings glad tidings! (How welcome is your coming that preaches the Good News of His good things!) –Rom. 10:15, AMP

Blessed (happy, fortunate, to be envied) are you, my child(ren), to whom the LORD imparts no iniquity and in whose spirit there is no deceit. –Psalm 32:2, AMP

There is no going into captivity for you and no cry of distress in your streets, precious child(ren)! For blessed are you of whom this is true; blessed are you whose God is the LORD. – Psalm 144:1:14

Even though you are young, child(ren), you are an example to the believers in speech, in conduct, in love, in faith, in purity. --I Tim. 4:12

Child(ren), you do not neglect the gift which is in you. – I Tim. 4:14

My child(ren), your tongue speaks of God's righteousness and praises all day long.—Psalm 35:26

You know the Truth, dear child(ren), and the Truth makes and keeps you free.–John 8:32

Dynamite child(ren), not many days from now you shall be baptized with (placed in, introduced to) the Holy Spirit. (And) you shall receive power (ability, efficiency, and might) when the Holy Spirit has come upon you, and you shall be God's witness to all the ends of the earth. —Acts 1:5, 1:8

Precious little one(s), the sharing of your faith produces and promotes full recognition and appreciation and understanding of every good (thing) that is ours in our identification with Christ Jesus (and unto His glory)—Phil.1:6, AMP

God's covenant with you, my child(ren), is to give you life and peace because of the (reverent and worshipful) fear with which (you, his priest) revere His Name and stand in awe of His Name. –Mal. 2:4-6, AMP

Child(ren), you have the mind of Christ (the Messiah) and do hold the thoughts (feelings and purposes) of His heart. –I Cor. 2:16, AMP

My precious child(ren), you (know and understand) what is the immeasurable and unlimited and surpassing greatness of His power in and for us who believe, as demonstrated in the working of His mighty strength. –Eph. 1:19, AMP

Even if some of these have negative connotations, as some Proverbs do, turn them around into positive proclamations for your children who are Godly seeds He's planting in this world! Blank pages follow as your worksheets and journal. (They will serve as a fascinating historical record of your journey with God!)

Now, you and your child(ren) write out these Scriptures on the next page, along with your thoughts about them:

Old Testament:
Ex. 23:30
Deut. 28:1-14; 30:19b, 20
Job 33:14, 15-19
Psalm. 20:1-5; 40:9,10; 57:9-11; 67:1, 2; 148:14
Prov. 10:6; 12:3b, 6b, 7b, 18b, 19a; 13:6a, 9a; 29:25
Song 6:8-9
Isa. 26:12; 30:19; 41:9; 54:13; 61:1-3
Dan. 11:32 NKJ
Joel 2:23-32

Zech. 4:6

Mal. 2:4-6

<u>New Testament</u>:

John 7:16, 7:38

Acts 4:33

Rom. 10:8

Eph. 1:19

Phil. 4:13

Col. 2:2-3, 6-7

I Pet. 1:2b

2 Pet. 1:2-10

Rev. 1:10-11

"'For I know the plans I have for you,' says the LORD, 'plans to prosper you and not to harm you, plans to give you a future and a hope.'" –Jer. 29:11

The next few pages have bonus materials for your family.

Remember, it is so important (and can create priceless, powerful keepsakes!) for you and/or your little ones to write your Scripture-prayers to God. With every year, these writings will become more precious to you! Use colored paper or notecards, journals, or whatever you like. Let the kid(s) illustrate with colors, markers, stickers—whatever gets them engaged!

Now, may the bonus material bless you also, to help you and your child(ren) to grow even closer to the LORD.

8 More Ways to Bless Your Kids

by Tonja Taylor[1] © 2019
previously published on FaithWriters.com

1. **Decisions - Let your kids make some**. I learned to ask my daughter (this was training from my career in sales), "Do you want to wear the red outfit or the blue one today?" and she would pick one. If she was hesitant, I would give her a few seconds and they say, "Pick one or I will decide for you." She would usually decide. For the past couple years, of course, she's often suggested a third option. And, if it's reasonable, I go with it—not just in apparel, but everything. "Do you want to eat an apple or grapefruit along with your cereal?" This also comes to deciding a new grocery item to buy one week, a new activity, a new movie to watch, etc.

2. **Ask them to help you make up a song or poem, especially silly ones**. My daughter and I have enjoyed working on humorous things. She is quite creative (even more after a college degree in graphic arts, and now that she's been happily married 4 years and will soon be 28)!

3. **Let them have a pet to learn responsibility.** My daughter had a puppy at her dad's, but we started with a fish at our house. She remembered to feed him every day, and learned to change out the water without (1) damaging the bowl, or (2) even more important, without damaging the fish. She also taught him various things, from Bible verses, to the denominations (not of churches) of money, and why they

---

1. http://www.faithwriters.com/member-profile.php?id=64826

all spend differently. He was taught that, should he ever need to choose among denominations, that it is always best to start with dollars. In addition, she taught her fish the planets, including the non-planet, Pluto, and reviewed them with him. She's even talked back and forth with him in Spanish....but she noticed that, no matter what the subject, he always seemed to have Mom's voice.

4. Now, where was I? Oh yes, **Allowances.** Not only financial payment for services rendered (more or less) by your little learner, but allowances in learning. As parents, we too must remember that we did not get everything right the first time, nor the second, nor sometimes the third......and sometimes we still don't. Most important is to teach your kids to tithe, no matter how young. For as Malachi 3:10-12[2] state, the first tenth (off the gross, not the net!) is the LORD's, and there are many blessings to obeying this command! After the tithe, we taught Victoria (and friends of hers we'd take church with us) to give offerings of the money she earns or is given. As a senior she learned to use a checking account and budget her money even more carefully. She likes to buy gifts for people, and that is good. However, we often explained to her that she is a gifted artist and writer, and an original drawing or writing by her is a welcome gift by many people—something we cannot buy. She was awarded scholarships every year through college, and did well!

5. **Teach them to use equipment,** carefully, and tell them that you know they are wise in using it. For instance, I started telling my daughter for years before she ever started driving that she was an excellent driver. She started on a

2. http://biblia.com/bible/esv/Malachi%203.10-12

riding lawn mower, going forward, backward, parallel parking, etc. And, once she got in a car, she was, of course, an excellent driver. I was very comfortable riding with her, from the start. She has even mentioned to me (years ago) that I the speed limit is "only 55" or that I should not drive in flip-flops. My teaching is coming back to me!

6. **Teach them to cook.** I started a bit too early with my daughter, and she is a great cook now. Her husband especially appreciates that. ☺

7. **Teach them to plant and tend a seed, then the plant, then harvest** the fruit, while imparting the spiritual lessons of sowing, patience, and reaping.

8. **Tell them every day—first thing, middle, last—how much you love them, that you are pleased with them, that you are thankful for them, and that they bring you great joy.** My daughter loved this till she became an older teen, and then it seemed to bother her, but I kept on. As a college grad and married adult, she has come back around, and never rolls her eyes. She now openly shows us that she likes to hear it. ☺ Anyway, we're going to keep saying it and she can't stop it from going in her ears! Be sure to remind them that, as much as you love them, God loves them even more!

More bonus material on the next pages!

7 Affirmations for Students

by Tonja Taylor[1] © 2021
previously published on FaithWriters.com

I don't remember if I told my fourth-graders in the small rural public school that the affirmations I had them say every morning were based on the Bible. I think it would have been a blessing to most of those sweeties, if they'd known that, but it may have created some problems with the administration.

However, almost every one of my students immediately loved doing this as a class, and most wanted to lead. I would have them stand, and, after we said the "Pledge of Allegiance", I would stand and say "The Daily Affirmations" God had given me with them.

My order of operations was that, during the nine weeks, every student would lead the class (even if they didn't want to; I'd let another student with whom they were friends stand with them if needed), usually several times.

Sometimes, a student would try to be funny, and say them too quickly, or in a high-pitched voice. It was a distraction, so when that happened, I'd have them start again. It didn't take long for the other kids to tell the distracting students to "Shut up!" and then we'd start again.

This is what the LORD led me to have them say:
Using my power of choice,
I control myself.
I show respect to myself and others.
I am wise, so I obey my leaders.
I am excellent.

---

1. http://www.faithwriters.com/member-profile.php?id=64826

82

I am trustworthy.
I am quick to help others.
I am special and loved, and I believe it.

All of these are based on the Word of God! I believe, because our Father God is so good, so all-knowing, so eager to bless us, that His Spirit overshadowed these words when my students spoke them in unison. I could see the heart in almost all of my students, every morning, as they said them. A couple were reluctant on some days—but they were still hearing them, and thus, those good seeds were being planted, and watered!

Another thing about the Word of God is that, once it's rooted in the heart, it remains! During the last few months of the year, my word processing program that worked with the interactive whiteboard was never repaired, even though I requested it. So, I came in one day and could not project the affirmations, as I had been doing for months, for the class to read.

However, a few students jumped up and eagerly volunteered to lead the class from memory! I was so blessed, and close to tears, as I saw and heard their eager hearts to lead their classmates in those inspiring words, with no writing on the board—for the affirmations were written in their hearts! Glory to God!

The LORD is so very faithful! He always puts His blessing on our genuine efforts to help others, even if they don't show appreciation. After all, He says in His Word that, when we do it to the "least of these," or "the littlest one," that we do it for Him. Praise Him, our good and kind and gracious, merciful, faithful Master Who loves us so much He died for us!

Ask the LORD today for strategies to draw your class or family closer to Christ. He will help you!

Keep reading—next is a prayer to say daily over your children!

A Powerful Prayer For Your Kids

©2021 by Tonja Taylor[1]
previously published by FaithWriters.com

I read Colossians 1:4-7 (AMPC) today, and realized I can make a prayer out of it for myself and my loved ones: **[4]For we have heard of your faith in Christ Jesus [the leaning of your entire human personality on Him in absolute trust and confidence in His power, wisdom, and goodness] and of the love which you [have and show] for all the saints (God's consecrated ones), [5]Because of the hope [of experiencing what is] laid up (reserved and waiting) for you in heaven. Of this [hope] you heard in the past in the message of the truth of the Gospel,**

[6]Which has come to you. Indeed, in the whole world [that Gospel] is bearing fruit *and* still is growing[by its own inherent power], even as it has done among yourselves ever since the day you first heard and came to know and understand the grace of God in truth. [You came to know the grace or undeserved favor of God in reality, deeply and clearly and thoroughly, becoming accurately and intimately acquainted with it.] [7]You so learned it from Epaphras, our beloved fellow servant. He is a faithful minister of Christ in our stead *and* as our representative *and yours*.

So I took most of verses 4 and 6, and slightly modified them to pray for my family and myself:

Thank You, LORD, that others hear of our faith in Christ Jesus [how we lean our whole lives on Him in absolute trust and confidence in His power, wisdom, and goodness] and of the love we have and show for all the saints (God's consecrated ones).

Thank You, LORD, that Your Good News is bearing fruit and growing [by its own inherent power], among us since the day we

1. http://www.faithwriters.com/member-profile.php?id=64826

first heard and came to know and understand the grace of God in truth. [We are coming to know the grace or undeserved favor of God in reality, deeply and clearly and thoroughly, becoming accurately and intimately acquainted with it.]

Hallelujah!

See how easy that is? You can use this, and most of the Scriptures in the Bible to pray over your family! Get started today, for the entrance of God's Word brings light (revelation, understanding):

The entrance and unfolding of Your words give light; their unfolding gives understanding (discernment and comprehension) to the simple.—Psalm 119:130 (AMPC)

His Word always accomplishes that for which He sends it (Isaiah 55:11-12)! Ask Him to guide you to the exact Scriptures to pray over your family and yourself. He is faithful. He loves to help people understand and benefit from His Word. Ask Him. He will help you!

From Sorrow to Shalom!

© 2024 by Tonja K. Taylor
Previously published on FaithWriters.com

³¹**What then shall we say to [all] this? If God is for us, who [can be] against us? [Who can be our foe, if God is on our side?] ³²He who did not withhold or spare [even] His own Son but gave Him up for us all, will He not also with Him freely and graciously give us all [other] things?**—Romans 8:31-32, AMPC

The LORD is so good to help us! Having to deal with my widowed mom's physical and mental afflictions through the years, and especially in the last intensely-challenged months of her life as my husband and I cared for her 24/7 (at the direction of God), the LORD revealed to me that, for almost 60 years, I'd been afflicted with grief and sorrow—which Jesus's blood broke the power of at the cross!

Most of the came down through family lines; generational curses, especially on my mother's side. Gee, she's been depressed since I've known her, although there have been bright moments of fleeting happiness, amazing creativity, lots of kindness and generosity, and deep compassion for us and others.

It takes to power of God to deliver people. Even Christians can know something is wrong, but not know how to fix it—and thus suffer condemnation, along with the rest of the junk. This was my story, until the LORD led me to churches and books and other teachings where I could discover the Truth.

As we grow in the knowledge of the Word of God, and as the Holy Spirit leads us (because only He knows what we can handle; what we are willing to confront and conquer, with His help!), we can take authority over the demons behind these wrong things that have oppressed us, and also lean on Daddy God for His Grace to overcome our fleshly bad habits—and never go back to them!

In [this] freedom Christ has made us free [and completely liberated us]; stand fast then, and do not be hampered *and* held ensnared *and* submit again to a yoke of slavery [which you have once put off]. – Galatians 5:1, AMPC

This will continue until we get to Heaven, because the dear Holy Spirit Who is Wisdom; Who is the Spirit of Truth, will always be leading us higher, to become more like the dear Savior Jesus Christ. Hallelujah!

For whom he did foreknow, he also did predestinate to be conformed to the image of his Son, that he might be the firstborn among many brethren. – Romans 8:29, KJV

So, becoming more like Jesus is quite a process, but He gives us His sweet Presence, through His Word, prayer, worship, and thankfulness to Him; focusing on Him on purpose, as He commands us.

I praise Him for His Word, and for the availability of the Word in written and audio and visual form, as well as true worship on the radio; my excellent Bible-believing church; and my strong Christian husband.

(I didn't always have all these things, but I had the Word, and, life gets gritty and real, it's the Word that saves us! I would take Scriptures such as these, as I've illustrated in *Legacy*, and personalize them. It was truly the washing of the water of the Word that gave me fresh breath and helped me "keep on keeping on"; that saved my mind and emotions and life—every time!)

So, just like I've taught you in *Legacy*, here are a few more examples of how the Word can be made personal: I would put my name in the Scripture, and speak it aloud (Sometimes at the top of my voice, if no human was around, or (mostly) in a low tone, or even whispers, as needed. The LORD hears our hearts, our whispers, and everything else, for His lovingkindness is better than life; His ear is ever attentive to us, His precious kids! Hallelujah!

So put your name in the Scripture(s) and speak it; it's for you! Here's how I did it; you can too!

I have told you these things (Tonja), so that in Me you may have [perfect] peace and confidence. In the world you have tribulation and trials and distress and frustration; but (Tonja) be of good cheer [take courage; be confident, certain, undaunted]! For I have overcome the world. [I have deprived it of power to harm you and have conquered it for you.] – John 16:33, AMPC

Now the mind of the flesh [which is sense and reason without the Holy Spirit] is death [death that comprises all the miseries arising from sin, both here and hereafter]. But (I, Tonja, have) the mind of the [Holy] Spirit (which, for me) is life and [soul] peace [both now and forever]. – Romans 8:6, AMPC

Now the God of peace, that brought again from the dead our Lord Jesus, that great shepherd of the sheep, through the blood of the everlasting covenant, make you perfect in every good work (Tonja) to do his will, working in you that which is well pleasing in his sight, through Jesus Christ; to whom be glory for ever and ever. Amen. - Hebrews 13:20-21, KJV

Thank the LORD that He sees the totality of our lives, and knows what we can become—for I would have given up on me a long time ago! However, we are never without His help, if we will just receive it. Hallelujah!

(Tonja), Let your character or moral disposition be free from love of money [including greed, avarice, lust, and craving for earthly possessions] and be satisfied with your present [circumstances and with what you have]; for He [God] Himself has said, (Tonja) I will not in any way fail you nor give you up nor leave you without support. [I will] not, [I will] not, [I will] not in any degree leave you helpless nor forsake nor let [you] down (relax My hold on you (Tonja))! [Assuredly not!]—Hebrews 13:5, AMPC

Praise our faithful Father God, and LORD Jesus our Savior, and the awesome, sweet Comforter, the dear Holy Spirit! They (Who are One) will never leave us; they are with us always! Wow and glory!

God said, Let Us [Father, Son, and Holy Spirit] make mankind in Our image, after Our likeness, and let them have complete authority... - Genesis 1:26, AMPC

And I will ask the Father, and He will give you another Comforter (Counselor, Helper, Intercessor, Advocate, Strengthener, and Standby), that He may remain with you forever—John 14:16, AMPC

The LORD has helped me understand, through much pain and trial and error, and other junk, that I've spent way too much of my time, energy, thought, and even money trying to please her and others that cannot really be pleased. So, through the trials with caring 24/7 for my dear disabled, diseased, depressed mother, He delivered me from much of that!

I love her, and she loves me, of course (At the time of this update, she's been in Heaven almost a year, finally with Dad and all of her family, including two babies she lost before I was born, that she never got to know. When the negative emotions from the enemy come, where he tries to put that grief and sadness and sorrow and regret and junk back on me, the LORD (My faithful Helper and Defender and Wisdom and Strong Tower and Refuge forever!) quickly reminds me to picture her and Dad (who went to Heaven about 7 years ago) free and happy and healed and whole, highly enjoying themselves—with "no more mad, no more sad; only glad memories" as I often sing, as I overcome and refocus on the positive!)

Through those hard years and last very difficult months (although the LORD's Grace always makes things certainly better than they would be without Him!), we proved our love for each other in covenant ways; when things were falling apart and the hardest, we've (my husband and me; he is my hero on earth!) been there for each other, as the LORD has orchestrated things. That is the root of true love: not abandoning those to whom you are attached, especially in the hardest of times.

Then, we cooperate with the LORD to work on our souls (mind, will, emotions). That's where the trouble is, for our spirits are united with Christ, and perfect, once we truly repent of our sins and receive Christ Jesus, the firstborn Son of God, the only Messiah, as our Savior and LORD, and thus become born again (Psalm 25:5, John 3:15-17, Romans 5:6, Hebrews 2:3)!

Remember—just put your name (and/or your child(ren) and/or other loved one(s) in the verse(s), wherever you feel led to. The Bible is God's unique Love Letter to each of us! Also, remember—the enemy (who forever lies!) will try to discourage you, and tell you that your declaration of the Word is not working. *But it is!* Things that seem to take so long to us are in God's timeless hands. He is always working (Genesis 50:20, Psalm 121:3, Isaiah 40:28, Romans 8:28, Ephesians 2:10 and 3:20)!

³Praised (honored, blessed) be the God and Father of our Lord Jesus Christ (the Messiah)! By His boundless mercy (I, Tonja) have been born again to an ever-living hope through the resurrection of Jesus Christ from the dead, ⁴[Born anew] into an inheritance which is beyond the reach of change and decay [imperishable], unsullied and unfading, reserved in heaven for you, (Tonja)- I Peter 1:3-4, AMPC

Everyone who believes (adheres to, trusts, and relies on the fact) that Jesus is the Christ (the Messiah) is a born-again child of God; and everyone who loves the Father also loves the one born of Him (His offspring). - I John 5:1, AMPC

Great is His faithfulness, amen—and, praise the LORD, He is never depressed! He is never angry, nor critical, nor condemning, nor double-minded, and many other things that humans often exhibit and others think is God.

As free, (I, Tonja, live) and not using your liberty for a cloak of maliciousness, but as the servants of God. - I Peter 2:16, KJV

Anyway, I really want to focus on the positive here, so let me do that: The LORD has liberated me! Hallelujah! He has made me much more glad than sad, and is helping me recognize and root out every little last root of wrong, of sorrow and sadness, so that the seeds of thanksgiving and peace and joy and more good things can grow and produce abundant fruit.

The LORD has done great things for us; (I, Tonja, and) we are filled with joy.– Psalm 126:3, Berean Standard Bible

He is so faithful and good, and continues to put His Grace all over my life, to continually reveal to me Who He is (which has, of course, been different in many ways that what most of us have experienced from parents, pastors, and other leaders in our lives!).

Through many traumatic events during the first few decades of my life, the LORD kept drawing me to Himself and His Word. Hallelujah! These things caused shame and unbelief and fear and doubt about my worth; my parents, I realized through the years, were experiencing the same, and had no idea how to truly, spiritually get victory over them. So, they did not know how to help me.

Because I was not grounded in the Word, nor stable in Bible-believing church attendance, prayer, or worship of Christ, I doubted whether I was really loved and accepted (even though there were several proofs that I was all these things, but not knowing how to really recognize nor defeat the doubt and unbelief and anxiety about that), these thoughts afflicted me for decades.

As I started learning more about the LORD in my early 20s, and drawing closer to Him, I started realizing after a point that this junk I was experiencing in various ways was different than what I was hearing preachers say about God, and different than I was reading about in the Word.

For by grace are ye saved through faith (Tonja); and that not of yourselves: it is the gift of God:- Ephesians 2:8, KJV

So, being born again is instant, praise the LORD, but the sanctification of working out our Salvation is a process which will only be completed in Heaven. So as He teaches us His Word and we agree with it and walk it in, we start having more of Heaven on earth—which was the Plan from the beginning (Genesis 1).

Wherefore seeing we also are compassed about with so great a cloud of witnesses, let us lay aside every weight, and the sin which doth so easily beset us, and let us run with patience the race that is set before us, Looking unto Jesus the author and finisher of our faith; who for the joy that was set before him endured the cross, despising the shame, and is set down at the right hand of the throne of God.- Hebrews 12:1-2, KJV

He taught me to worship Him in spirit and truth. Hallelujah! He has truly freed me and turned my mourning into dancing and my sorrow into shalom!

He wants to do the same for you and your child(ren). It was never His will for any of us to experience evil. There is no sickness, sin, nor sorrow or other negative in Heaven, and it is possible, with His help and Grace, to have days of Heaven on earth, by learning how to cultivate true peace (Shalom) in our bodies and souls! Ask Him today; cry out to Him, and He will help you! He is faithful, gracious, merciful, and always willing to help you!

Now I know that the LORD rescues (me, Tonja) his anointed king. He will answer (me) him from his holy heaven and rescue (me) him by his great power. - Psalm 20:6, NLT

Blessed be the LORD, because he hath heard the voice of my (Tonja's) supplications. The LORD is my strength and my shield; my heart trusted in him, and I am helped: therefore my heart greatly rejoiceth; and with my song will I praise him. - Psalm 28:6¹-7, KJV

About the Author

Tonja K. Taylor and her husband Clayton live to exalt the true God, the LORD Jesus Christ.

Tonja has a mandate to teach others through books, presentations, and more, to help them experience Christ. She has enjoyed many God-breathed adventures from teaching and championing kids for over 40 years, in church; schools; online tutoring students in the USA and 8 other countries; in community organizations in the USA. Her experiences in ministry, business, education, and the fine arts allow her to bring a multi-faceted approach to her work, so that her audiences are engaged, enriched, and empowered as they learn—providing them with an amazing amount of value for their investment.

Tonja and her heroic husband live to glorify LORD Jesus, our soon-returning King! They serve in various capacities at Eagle Mountain International Church in Texas.

Check out their "River Rain Creative" (300+ videos) and "POWERLight Learning" You Tube channels:
https://www.youtube.com/@riverraincreative599/videos
https://www.youtube.com/@POWERLightLearning-qu7tn/videos

Read about faith, worship, prayer, divine health, life's funnies, and more: 1,250+ articles by Tonja on FaithWriters.com: https://www.faithwriters.com/member-profile.php?id=64826, and also enjoy Tonja's older *Legacy* podcasts: https://www.podchaser.com/podcasts/rainwater-2441681/episodes/recent#[1]

We know you can speak the Word over your child(ren), and shape their lives for Christ! You'll never go wrong speaking the Word of God. He can take even one Scripture spoken in faith, and do great things with it!

---

1.   https://www.podchaser.com/podcasts/rainwater-2441681/episodes/recent

Even when it seems like nothing is happening, God is working! As Isaiah 65:23, KJV, states: **"They shall not labour in vain, nor bring forth for trouble; for they are the seed of the blessed of the LORD, and their offspring with them."** Hallelujah!

God bless in your ZOE life with our loving Father and LORD!
Thank you for your prayers and purchases, and for loving God and sharing the Good News of Christ!

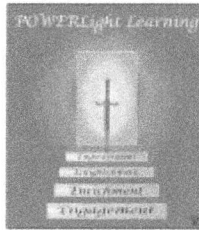

Don't miss out!

Visit the website below and you can sign up to receive emails whenever Tonja K. Taylor publishes a new book. There's no charge and no obligation.

https://books2read.com/r/B-A-HSCAB-GXOHG

BOOKS 2 READ

Connecting independent readers to independent writers.

Did you love *The New Legacy Expanded*? Then you should read *POWERLight Lit Tips for Better Teaching*[2] by Tonja K. Taylor!

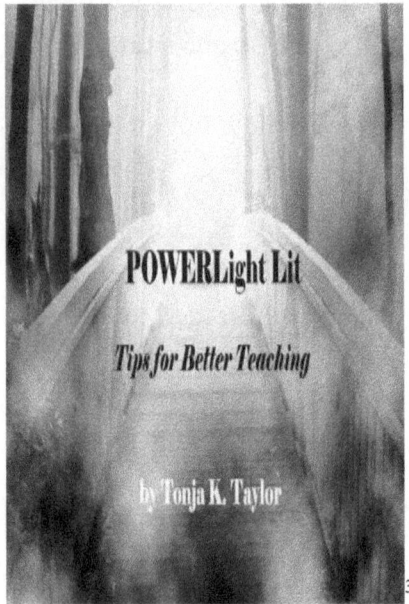

POWERLight Lit Tips for Better Teaching is a quick, powerful read of Tonja's decades of multi-faceted experiences in ministry, education, business, and the fine arts. She shares tips and techniques, God-breathed and otherwise, to help educators, parents, pastors, and other influencers be more effective in teaching--whether to our own child(ren), or to diverse groups in school, church, community, online, and more! Ultimately, God is the Teacher, and we are His vessels. May His words flow through us to cause us to be catalysts for positive change!

---

2. https://books2read.com/u/mgBGxq

3. https://books2read.com/u/mgBGxq

About the Author

"But when He, the Spirit of Truth, comes, He will guide you into all the truth [full and complete truth]. For He will not speak on His own initiative, but He will speak whatever He hears [from the Father—the message regarding the Son], and He will disclose to you what is to come [in the future]." - John 16:13, AMP

We need the Holy Spirit, Who is the Truth and always tells us the Truth, every day! While there are some fantasy elements in a few of these writings, they are all based on the Truth. May they bring you delight and insight, to the Glory of Jesus Christ--Who is the Way, the Truth, and the Life!

Read more at https://www.faithwriters.com/member-profile.php?id=64826.

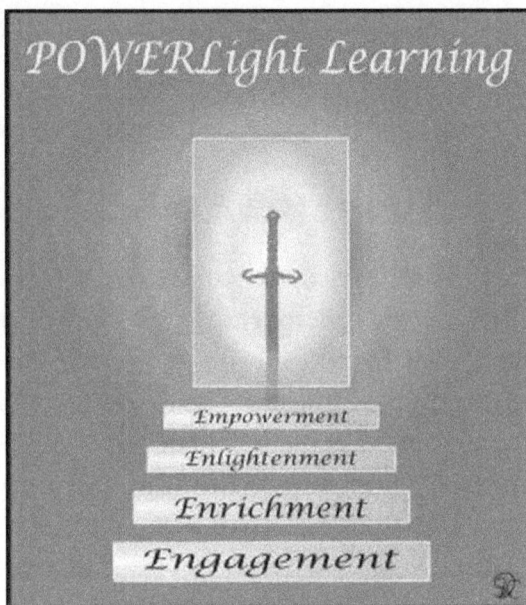

POWERLight Learning

Empowerment
Enlightenment
Enrichment
Engagement

About the Publisher

Through engagement and enrichment comes enlightenment and empowerment—for bad or for good.

The book publishing arm of POWERLight Learning is based on Romans 5:19 and 12:2, and engages, enriches, enlightens, and empowers readers through positively provocative works for good, for God; *"Because what you read matters!"*

As the eternal, infallible, unchanging Word of God states: *"**For the kingdom of God consists of and is based on not talk but power (moral power and excellence of soul).**"* - I Corinthians 4:20, AMPC

It is our prayer that works by POWERLight Learning will draw all who experience them to a deeper love and loyalty to the LORD Jesus Christ, our soon-returning King!

Read more at https://www.faithwriters.com/member-profile.php?id=64826.

www.ingramcontent.com/pod-product-compliance
Lightning Source LLC
Chambersburg PA
CBHW021206020426
42331CB00003B/222